HEMINGWAY IN MICHIGAN

HEMINGWAY IN MICHIGAN

by
Constance Cappel Montgomery

FLEET PUBLISHING CORPORATION
NEW YORK

To
ADAM DENISON CAPPEL
*And those for whom northern Michigan
was more than "just a place."*

Contents

SECTION I:
CHILDHOOD AND ADOLESCENCE

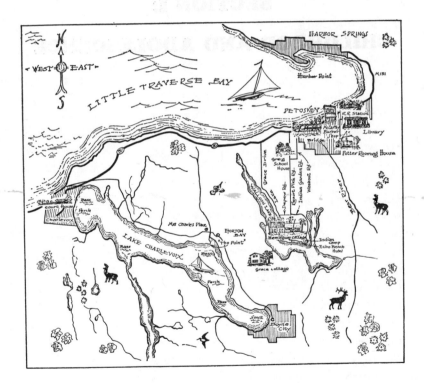

The Michigan Years

Ernest Hemingway first went to northern Michigan at the
turn of the century, as a one-year-old taken by his parents
to Walloon Lake. For many summers to come, the Hemingway family made the first leg of the journey to their
summer home by lake steamer from Chicago to Harbor
Springs, Michigan, on Little Traverse Bay.

Northern Michigan, a land of low, rolling hills heavily
forested with pines, maples, and birches, dotted with clear
lakes and ponds, is bordered to the west by the inland sea
which is Lake Michigan. Lumbering camps, steamboats
and working schooners, horse-drawn farm wagons, a pioneer life that Hemingway saw and partially shared as a
boy, no longer exist. The land looks the same, and the
wildness of the storms over the lake and the predominance
of weather over the lives of the people remains; but today
superhighways stretch upwards from Detroit towards the
sprawling bridge that crosses the Straits of Mackinac.
People from the cities seek their rest in much greater
numbers than in the early 1900's, and the life of northern
Michigan is more gauged to them than to the land. Hemingway loved this country.

Although many of the places in Michigan which Hemingway knew have changed, much of the countryside
described in his Michigan short stories and in the one
novel with a Michigan setting, *The Torrents of Spring,* is

exactly the same. Although always an acute and accurate reporter, in his early writings he became as autobiographical as any writer of fiction can be. Many of the people, as well as the places, described in his writings existed and still can be found. A farmhouse may have burned down, but the farmer who owned it will reminisce; a young Indian girl may be dead for many years, but she remains in the memory of others. From Hemingway's own past and memories came his Michigan writings, and from these writings in turn the pattern of his early life is revealed. Northern Michigan is where he knew his first love, where he first seriously practiced writing, and where he lived when he returned from the First World War.

Harbor Springs, Michigan, in 1898 (approximately when the Hemingways first came to the region) was emerging from a rough, pioneer lumber town into one of the most exclusive summer resorts in the United States. While the Eastern robber barons were building their castles of marble and stone in Newport, the wealthy industrialists of Detroit, Cincinnati, Lansing, St. Louis, and Chicago were building forty-room frame "cottages" on Harbor Point, a peninsula jutting into Little Traverse Bay.

Harbor Springs has probably changed less since Hemingway's infancy than any other town of the northern Michigan area he knew. The village grew quickly with the aid of the incoming wealth, and the same wealth, now in its fourth generation, has preserved the town as it was. In 1898 the lake steamers from Chicago would churn out of Lake Michigan into Little Traverse Bay, cross it, steam around Harbor Point, and drop anchor at Harbor Springs, the deepest natural harbor of the Great Lakes.

A spur of the Grand Rapids & Indiana Railroad connected the towns of Harbor Springs and Petoskey, eleven miles apart around the bay. The Hemingway family would carry their luggage from the dock to the train for the ride to Petoskey. As Doctor Hemingway and his family left the small, frame railroad station in Harbor Springs (which still stands), they probably enjoyed the view of the placid harbor protected by Harbor Point, with the clear and varicolored blue water of Little Traverse Bay beyond. The train would pass the dunes at the foot of the bay and rumble through Bay View, another resort. At Petoskey they again had to transfer their luggage and change cars for the train going to the village at Walloon Lake, then Bear Lake.

The view from the train window would be similar to the one now seen from the window of an automobile. Far out on Lake Michigan an ore carrier now leaves behind a stream of smoke, as the large side-wheelers once did. Closer into shore the waves still beat on the rock shoals, and birch and pine trees bend with the wind on shore. Petoskey, the small town at the curve of the bay, still stairsteps up the hills to the clear northern sky.

Petoskey, the setting of Hemingway's first published novel, *The Torrents of Spring*, remains the small town he knew with many of the same people living and working there. The rooming house on State Street where he lived and wrote in 1919 still stands. The daughter of the original owner lives in the house and likes to talk about her family's famous guest, who was an unknown writer when he lived there. Many other people living in Petoskey also like to talk about the Ernest Hemingway they knew as a boy and a young man.

The highway out of Petoskey towards Charlevoix goes past a dirt road. This road rises over the hills away from Little Traverse Bay to Walloon Lake and was described in the story "Ten Indians." Set deep in the trees on Walloon Lake is the Hemingway cottage where Ernest spent all of his summers from his first to his twenty-first year, except for the summer of 1918, when he was in Italy. One of his sisters still uses the cottage as her summer home.

With rolling hills surrounding it, Walloon Lake is considered one of the most beautiful of the smaller lakes in Michigan, but its character has changed since the days when Ernest Hemingway lived there. What was a rough outdoor setting for the Hemingway family is now a luxurious resort area where the "log cabins" sometimes run to twenty rooms. The lumber camp where the Indians worked and lived is gone as are the Indians who lived there. The steamers on Walloon Lake, which used to bring the Hemingways to their summer home, have disappeared.

Not far from Walloon Lake, on the road between Boyne City and Charlevoix, is the little town of Horton Bay which was the setting for the stories, "Up in Michigan," "The Three-Day Blow," and "The End of Something." The town was named for its first settler, Samuel Horton. It has changed little since the days when Hemingway fished in Horton's Creek, lived at the Dilworths' house, and eventually married there. With its neat, frame houses painted white, Horton Bay is the only locale in Hemingway's Michigan which has remained virtually untouched by tourists.

Ernest Hemingway was born on July 21, 1899. (He added a year to his age to obtain a job on the Kansas City *Star*, so that his birth date is often erroneously given as July 21, 1898.) With their young daughter and son, Marcelline and Ernest, Doctor and Mrs. Hemingway stayed at the Echo Beach Hotel (which has since burned down) before they built their summer cottage about a mile down the shore of Bear Lake (now called Walloon Lake).

Philip Young in his book about Hemingway observed that "the parts of the childhood which stuck were the summertimes, which were spent in Michigan."[1] The "summertimes" and even the other times of the year spent in Michigan did stick with Hemingway, and he used Michigan as the setting for ten published stories, sections of two other stories, one high school story (which only appeared previously in an Oak Park High School publication and is included in this book), and a short novel.

Ernest's older sister, Marcelline, remembered from what her parents told her that they first went to Walloon Lake in August, 1898, when she was seven months old. The Hemingways liked Walloon on their first visit and bought four lots, equalling one acre.

Ernest's younger brother, Leicester, who was sixteen years younger than Ernest and also had gathered the information from his parents, remembered it differently:

> *During the summer of 1900 our parents visited Walloon Lake in northern Michigan and were seized with a strange sense of shared destiny. They bought a tract of land—two acres of shore line more than four miles from the foot of the lake, which was then known as Bear Lake.*[2]

According to Owen White, whose family camped on the property next to the Hemingways', the Hemingway cottage, which was called "Windemere," was built by 1904, when Ernest was five. The Hemingway cottage has changed superficially, but not basically, since Ernest lived there. His sister, Madelaine "Sunny" Hemingway Miller, who still spends her summers there, explained: "This place isn't anything like it was when Ernie lived here. It was made of rough timber and had a porch. I closed in the breezeway. There wasn't any heat or electricity back when we came up with our father." She added, "Everything around here has changed so much that Ernie probably wouldn't be able to find his old fishing spots over at Horton Bay."

When the cottage was built, according to the late Marcelline Hemingway Sanford, it included only a living room with a large brick fireplace, a dining room, kitchen, two bedrooms, and a roofed-over porch. The exterior of the cottage was covered with white clapboard and the interior with white pine. A kitchen wing was added, and finally the cottage had six bedrooms, three in an annex.

Until 1917 Ernest lived an outdoor life during the summers in Michigan. When he was about sixteen, he had his first love affair, with an Indian girl in the Michigan woods. During the summer of 1917, when he became eighteen, Hemingway wanted to enlist in the Army, but he had damaged his eye when he was fourteen, while taking boxing lessons in Chicago, and was rejected. Instead of going to college in the autumn of 1917, Ernest went to Kansas City and worked as a reporter on the Kansas City *Star*. He was a reporter there until the spring of 1918, when he decided to join the volunteer ambulance unit of the Italian Army under the auspices of the American Red Cross. On April 30, 1918, he drew his last paycheck from the *Star* and returned to northern Michigan for a final fishing trip before going overseas. Carl Edgar, a Horton Bay friend who had worked for a fuel oil company in Kansas City and had shared an apartment there with Ernest during the winter of 1918, and Charlie Hopkins, the Kansas City *Times's* assignment editor, accompanied him.[3] Hemingway's orders were forwarded from Kansas City to Horton Bay, and he left hastily for New York City still wearing his fishing clothes.

On May 12 he was issued a uniform and was enlisted as an honorary lieutenant in the Italian Army. In late May of 1918 he sailed for Europe. Serving on the Italian front as an ambulance driver, he went through some of the bitterest fighting of the War. Badly wounded at Fossalta di Piave, Ernest was hospitalized at Milan and decorated by the Italians with their most coveted medal, the Medaglia d'Argento al Valore Militare, equivalent to the French Medaille Militaire; and with three Croci al Merito di Guerra.

After the War, Hemingway returned to the United

States on January 21, 1919, to recuperate. Since he had been injured at night, Ernest was not able to sleep in the dark for a long time. He went to Michigan in March of that year and then lived with his family off and on during the following summer. At this time he became emotionally involved with a girl from Petoskey who was fictionalized in several of his stories. In the fall he remained in Horton Bay at the Dilworths' house and picked potatoes for a living. He moved to Petoskey during the winter of 1919–1920 where he lived at Potter's Rooming House at 602 State Street. Hazel Potter, who was working in nearby Mancelona that winter, remembers that when she was home visiting on weekends, she often heard Hemingway "typing away all the time in his front corner room."

"I put in a fall and half a winter writing up in Petoskey, Michigan," Hemingway said many years later, describing the extent of the preparation which preceded his first expatriate publication in 1923. It was a period of discouraging rejection. "I worked and wrote," he said on another occasion, "and couldn't sell anything."[4]

During this winter, Hemingway concentrated on his writing, but he also visited and had dinner with many Petoskey friends. At the Pailthorp's, Hemingway met Ralph Connable, a personable American who headed Woolworth of Canada. In an interview with Frances Pailthorp, William Forrest Dawson wrote, "Connable asked about taking 'Dutch' Pailthorp back to Toronto with him. Dutch couldn't go himself, so he suggested his pal, Ernest."[5] Hemingway did not want to go back to his family in Chicago, so that about halfway through the winter he went to Toronto as a tutor for Connable's young son. Hemingway lived with the Connables in Toronto, and through Ralph Connable got his job with the Toronto *Star*, which subsequently took him back to Europe.

Returning to Michigan for the summer and early autumn of 1920, Ernest gathered material for the fishing and camping series which was published in the Toronto *Star Weekly*. His twenty-first birthday, which proved to be an eventful one, occurred during that summer.

In the fall of 1920, Hemingway went back to Chicago, where he lived in an apartment on the North Side, and it was there that he met Sherwood Anderson. He obtained a job editing the house organ of the Co-operative Society of America. While he lived in Chicago, he met Hadley Richardson, who was to become his first wife.

In September of 1921, Hemingway returned to Michigan for his last long visit. (Hemingway made only brief trips to Michigan after 1921.) On September 3, 1921, he married Hadley Richardson. After a two-week honeymoon at the Hemingway cottage on Walloon Lake, the couple moved to Chicago, then to Toronto, and finally to Paris.

Many of the more important events of Hemingway's formative years occurred in Michigan. He did his real growing up in northern Michigan, where he learned to fish, hunt, drink, know girls, and even to concentrate seriously on his writing. Hemingway, like one of the migratory birds which he hunted, always returned to Michigan in the summer. When he returned to the United States after being wounded in the First World War, he withdrew into himself like a hurt animal and healed his wounds in the solitude of a boarding house in Petoskey. When he took his therapeutic fishing trips, he fished in northern Michigan streams. Finally, when he found the woman to be his wife, he married her in Horton Bay, Michigan. The pattern is one of almost compulsive return to the home of the growing writer, Ernest Hemingway.

History of Northern Michigan

The history of northern Michigan embraces Indian wars, French and British occupation, frontier expansion, and the rough-and-tumble of lumbering days. A sense of this past was captured in Hemingway's Michigan writings —a past which Hemingway came to know, for he was a witness to the last years of the lumbering era. The Hemingway family lived each summer in a rough cottage, much as the first Michigan pioneers had lived before them. From his Indian friends he learned what it was to lead a frontier existence.

The Indians in northern Michigan encountered by Jean Nicolet, a French explorer who passed through the Straits of Mackinac in 1634, were of the same tribes Hemingway knew more than two and a half centuries later, the Ottawas and Chippewas (the English name for the Indian word, Ojibwas), tribes of the Algonquin family. The place of origin of the Ottawas is obscure, but it is generally assumed that the tribe came from the east, advanced up the Ottawa River in Canada, then moved westward off the north shore of Lake Huron and passed by the Manitoulin Islands. At Sault Sainte Marie they first met the Chippewas, who inhabited the country bordering on Lake Superior. The two tribes were surprised to find that, although neither had known of the existence of the other, their languages were so similar that they were able to converse.

A loose confederacy was established between the Ottawas, Chippewas, and Potawatamis, and they became known as The Three Brothers. These tribes held undisputed possession of nearly the whole lower peninsula of Michigan.

In 1668 Father Jacques Marquette established the first permanent settlement in Michigan at the foot of the rapids on what is now the American side of the Sault Sainte Marie. He was sent to New France to be a missionary among the Ottawas. An Indian war among the Sioux, the Hurons, and the Ottawas, in which the Sioux tribe was victorious, drove Father Marquette to Michilimackinac and finally to what was to be named St. Ignace. In 1671 he established a mission, named after St. Ignatius, which was the first white settlement at the Straits of Mackinac.

A letter written by Marquette in 1671 describes the region which Hemingway's Nick Adams later passes through in the story "Big Two-Hearted River."

> *Michilimackinac is an island, famous in these regions, of more than a league in diameter, elevated in some places by such high cliffs as to be seen more than twelve leagues off. It is situated just in the strait forming the communication between Lake Huron and Illinois* [Lake Michigan]. *It is the key and, as it were, the gate for all the tribes from the south, as the Sault is for those of the north, there being in this section of country only those two passages by water; for a great number of nations have to go by* [one] *or other of these channels, in order to reach the French settlements.*[1]

Father Marquette remained with the mission at St. Ignace for about two years and exercised control over the Indians living in the area of northern Michigan where Hemingway later lived. Marquette wanted to explore the Mississippi and on May 17, 1673, left St. Ignace with the explorer Louis Jolliet and five men. The co-discoverers of the Mississippi followed it as far as what is now Arkansas, determining that the river must empty into the Gulf of Mexico. Returning up the river, Father Marquette was stricken with dysentery, from which he had previously suffered; and fearing that he was going to die, he set out, from the present vicinity of Chicago, for St. Ignace.

On May 18, 1675, Father Marquette died at the age of thirty-eight—some scholars believe on the shore of what is now called the Betsie River in southern Michigan—hundreds of miles from St. Ignace. Father Claude Dablon, Father Marquette's superior at Quebec, wrote about Marquette's last day on earth. Father Dablon's words reveal Marquette's character and give an understanding of why Marquette's name and reputation were so great in his own day and still linger among the people of the northland where he traveled and taught:

> *The evening before his death, which was a Friday, he told them, very joyously, that it would take place on the morrow. He conversed with them during the whole day as to what would need to be done for his burial: about the manner in which they should inter him; of the spot that should be chosen for his grave; how his feet, his hands, and his face should be arranged; how they should erect a Cross over his grave. He even went so far as to counsel them, 3 hours before he expired, that as soon as he was dead they should take the little Hand-bell of his Chapel, and sound it while he was being put underground. He spoke of all these things with so great tranquility and presence of mind that one might have supposed that he was concerned with the death and funeral of some other person, and not with his own.*[2]

Two years later a party of Ottawa Indians whom Marquette had instructed visited his grave. They exhumed the body and prepared it according to tribal custom. They then put the remains in a birchbark box and set out for the mission at St. Ignace. Nearly thirty canoes formed the funeral procession, the Iroquois joining the Algonquins, which lent more honor to the ceremonial. The fact that the Ottawa Indians let their traditional enemies, the Iroquois, join them in order to pay tribute to Father Marquette shows how much the peace-making priest was revered. At St. Ignace the Indians bearing Father Marquette's remains were received with solemn ceremony. The birchbark coffin was buried in the chapel which Marquette had built, in a vault next to the altar where he had officiated.

Father Marquette was one of the first missionaries to bring Catholicism to northern Michigan. For the next two centuries Catholic priests endured the hardships of the land, and to this day almost all of the Indians in the area are Catholics.

Although none of Hemingway's family was Catholic, the Indians he grew up with were. Hemingway did not become a Catholic until after he had been wounded in Italy, and even then he was not a baptized member of the faith. But Hemingway's religious sympathies had their roots in the religion that Father Marquette first brought to the Indians of northern Michigan.

The Chippewas were allies of the French in their colonial wars with England which broke out in 1744 after years of unrest. In the period which elapsed between the defeat of the French in 1760 and the Treaty of Paris in 1763, much anti-British feeling was aroused among all of the Indians. The English were arrogant towards the Indians, gave them no presents, and tried instead to cheat them out of their scanty acquisitions. The French, meanwhile, inflamed the Indians and impressed them with the belief that the English were their deadly enemies. The Chippewas, filled with hatred for the English and naturally warlike fell in with the schemes of the Ottawa chief, Pontiac, and took the lead in the massacre at Fort Mackinac in 1763. The French, who were on good terms with the Chippewas, were unharmed. The Ottawas did not take part in the massacre.

Alexander Henry, one of the first English traders to go among the Indians, was at the fort during the massacre, the bloodiest battle between Indians and white men in the history of northern Michigan. He lived to write about his experiences and described the difference between the two tribes and the location of their villages at the time of the massacre.

> *The Indians near Michilimackinac were the Objib-was* [sic] *and Ottawas, the former of whom claimed the eastern section of Michigan, and the latter the western, their respective portions being separated by a line drawn southward from the fort itself. The principal village of the Objibwas contained about a hundred warriors, and stood on the island of Michilimackinac, now called Mackinac. There was another smaller village near the head of Thunder Bay. The Ottawas, to the number of two hundred and fifty warriors lived at the settlement of L'Arbre Croche, on the shores of Lake Michigan, some distance southwest of the fort. This place was then the seat of the old Jesuit mission of St. Ignace, originally placed by Father Marquette on the northern side of the Straits. Many of the Ottawa were nominal Catholics. They were all somewhat improved from their original savage condition, living in log houses, and cultivating corn and vegetables to such an extent as to supply the fort with provision, besides satisfying their own wants. The Objibwas, on the other hand, were not in the least degree removed from their primitive barbarism.*[3]

Alexander Henry relates that the Ojibwas played a game of ball called "baggatiway" outside the gates of the fort. About four hundred Indians were engaged in the game, while the inhabitants of the fort, both soldiers and Canadians, numbered about ninety. The noise of the game diverted the officers and men and permitted the Indians to take the fort. The English soldiers were strolling around outside the fort without weapons and did not realize, until they heard the first shrill war whoop, that the slaughter had begun in the midst of the four hundred Indians supposedly chasing the ball.

Henry had not gone to the game, but instead was writing letters at his lodging within the fort. When he heard the war whoop, he grabbed the only available gun, a fowling piece filled with swan shot, and ran to a window, too late to stop an Indian from scalping an Englishman who was still alive. He continued to watch the massacre and noticed that the Canadians were not attacked. The British trader immediately left his lodging by the back door, climbed over a fence, and went into the next-door neighbor's house. The neighbor, a French-Canadian named M. Langlade, was calmly watching the slaughter with his family when Henry begged him for refuge. Langlade shrugged his shoulders and said, "Que voudriez-vous que j'en ferais?" Luckily, a slave of Langlade, a Pawnee woman, felt sorry for Henry and led him to a room in the garret, where she locked him in and took away the key.

From his garret room Henry watched the massacre.

Through an aperture, which afforded me a view of the area of the fort, I beheld, in shapes the foulest and most terrible, the ferocious triumphs of barbarian conquerors. The dead were scalped and mangled; the dying were writhing and shrieking, under the unsatiated knife and tomahawk; and from the bodies of some, ripped open, their butchers were drinking the blood, scooped up in the hollow of joined hands, and quaffed amid shouts of rage and victory. I was shaken, not only with

*horror, but with fear. The sufferings which I witnessed,
I seemed on the point of experiencing. No long time
elapsed before, every one being destroyed who could be
found, there was a general cry of All is finished.*[4]

Henry was captured by the Ojibwas, but, through a
series of reprieves from death, eventually was saved by the
Ottawas. (The Ottawas believed the Ojibwas had insulted
them by destroying the English at Fort Mackinac without
consulting the brother tribe.) The Ojibwas were taking
him and other English prisoners in canoes to the Isles of
Castor (Beaver Island and the islands surrounding it)
when they were tricked ashore by the Ottawas. The
Ottawas then took the fort from the Ojibwas, and soon
Henry was safely on his way to Montreal.

From the time of the massacre at Fort Mackinac until
the War of 1812, little of historical import happened in the
area of Michigan Hemingway later wrote about. Although
Michigan had become a state in 1805, the only inhabitants
of this region were the Ottawas and the missionaries who
lived among them. During the American Revolution the
post at Michilimackinac had been occupied by a British
garrison. Although the Treaty of Paris of 1783 terminated
the war and provided for Michilimackinac's surrender to
the United States, British troops remained in control of
the fort until July, 1796, following Jay's Treaty of 1794
which clearly established the Northwest Territory as an
American possession. Later, during the War of 1812, the
British, with the help of both the Ottawas and Chippewas,
captured Mackinac Island again. Two years later the
Americans attempted to retake the fort, and many were
slain. In the winter of 1814–15, when peace was con-
cluded, the British evacuated the post, and the American
troops took peaceable possession.

The Ottawas continued to live on the Lake Michigan
shoreline from Mackinaw City to Harbor Springs until

about 1840, when over half of the Indians moved to Canada because they feared being moved to Western reservations by the United States Government. Around 1827 the Catholics moved their mission from Seven Mile Point to Little Traverse, now Harbor Springs, and built a church of cedar logs. Not until 1853 were year-round, white residents living at Little Traverse. Before then the traders from Mackinac brought goods down to the Indians living near the mission. Several fishermen and a number of tradesmen formed the first permanent white population of Little Traverse.

In 1875–76 all the lands around Little Traverse Bay were thrown open to settlement. Soon farms were cleared in the forest. Real-estate and professional men moved into offices in the new, frame buildings of Little Traverse. Docks were built, sawmills went up, and several newspapers were started. By 1880 the railroad connected the little town with Petoskey, and by 1881 Little Traverse was incorporated as the village of Harbor Springs. The village began growing as a resort center, beginning with the formation of the Harbor Point Association. Hemingway, in his story "Ten Indians" described seeing the lights of Harbor Springs at night over Little Traverse Bay.

The city of Petoskey, the setting of Hemingway's short novel, *The Torrents of Spring*, was named for a Chippewa Indian, Pe-to-se-ga. Pe-to-se-ga, which means "the Rising Sun," was given the first name of Ignatius by the Catholic missionaries when he was born in 1787. But when Ignatius Pe-to-se-ga became a chief, he decided to send his two oldest sons to a Protestant school in northern Ohio. The Catholic priests in the Little Traverse mission then excommunicated him, which precipitated many changes in his life. First he moved to the present location of Petoskey, and then his wife, who was a staunch Catholic, left him. Undaunted, Pe-to-se-ga took another wife, had fourteen children by her, worshipped in a nearby Protestant mission with his children, and lived to be ninety-four years old.

In 1873 a white man built the first house in Petoskey, and by 1875 the community had grown to 118 houses, ten stores, six saloons, three hotels, two churches, and a blacksmith shop. Petoskey became incorporated as a city in 1896 and became the seat of Emmet County in 1902, several years after the Hemingway family had started building their nearby summer home.

The wild, lumbering days in Michigan began about 1872, and by the turn of the century most of the pine forests were gone. Cadillac, which was mentioned in Hemingway's "The Light of the World," was typical of the lumbering boomtowns in northern Michigan. In 1872 Cadillac was a crude railroad station on the Grand Rapids & Indiana line in the midst of a dense pine forest stretching in all directions. Twenty years later Cadillac was a flourishing city of over 4,500 people, but the pine forests surrounding it were gone.

Many sections of northern Michigan which Hemingway knew and wrote about still seem to be a wilderness, with their second-growth forests, isolated lakes, and untouched streams. The flavor of the end of the nineteenth century is still intact in towns such as Harbor Springs and Horton Bay. The past lingers in this historically important area, which the first Europeans discovered at about the same time the Pilgrims reached Plymouth.

Grandparents and Early Memories

Until he was five years old, Ernest Hemingway, with his parents and three of his sisters (Marcelline, Ursula, and Madelaine), lived in his maternal Grandfather Hall's house in Oak Park, Illinois, a suburb of Chicago. Ernest Hall (for whom Hemingway was named) lived at 439 North Oak Park Avenue, and directly across the street at 444 North Park Avenue lived Ernest's Grandmother and Grandfather Hemingway.

Doctor Hemingway, Ernest's father, did not seem to mind the arrangement, because Grandmother Caroline Hancock Hall had died several years earlier leaving Ernest Hall by himself in the large house, and Grandfather Hall went to California in the winters, leaving the Hemingway family free to run the household as they pleased. During the summers the Hemingways went to Walloon Lake, so that only in the spring and fall did all three generations occupy the large house on North Park Avenue.

In the story "Now I Lay Me" the main character, Nick Adams, had been wounded. Some nights, in order to go to sleep and forget his pain, Nick tried to think of the earliest thing he could remember, which was the attic of the house where he was born. In this attic there were jars of snakes and other specimens his father had collected as a boy and had preserved in alcohol.

Nick Adams was remembering an attic like the one in Ernest Hemingway's early home, the house of his Grandfather Hall. Marcelline, Ernest's older sister, also remembered: "Within the little tower was a circular room, a part of the attic, where my young doctor-father kept his medical specimens on high shelves out of the reach of us children."[1]

In "Now I Lay Me," Nick Adams's early memories of things (the jars of snakes in alcohol) lead to other childhood memories (the actions of his mother towards his father and his father's reactions). Nick remembers that after his grandfather died, his own family had moved to a new house designed and built by his mother.

The Hemingways moved to their own house when Ernest was five, after Grandfather Hall died. Mrs. Hemingway had inherited enough money from her father to build the house she wanted. "She designed its fifteen rooms, including a thirty-by-thirty music room two stories high with a balcony . . ."[2]

Then Nick remembers that, when they moved to the new house, the jars of specimens were burned in the backyard, but he cannot remember who had burned the snakes. Nick does remember, though, who burned his father's arrowheads and other treasures: his mother. In the story, while his father is gone on a hunting trip, his mother cleans out the basement in the "new house." When his father comes home, he discovers the fire. He asks Nick to get a rake and then carefully rakes from the ashes stone axes, stone skinning knives, pieces of pottery, and shattered arrowheads. Nick's mother goes into the house, and Nick and his father are left together with the ruined collection. The mother-father relationship is similar to the one outlined in the story "The Doctor and the Doctor's Wife."

Again the interests of Ernest's father parallel those of Nick's father, for Doctor Hemingway had spent his free hours as a boy delving into Indian mounds along the Des Plaines River. His daughter Marcelline wrote: "He hunted for arrowheads, clay bowls, spearheads and other remnants of Indian life for his growing collection of Indian artifacts. He found some stone ax heads, and he had a remarkable collection of flints which he showed to us when we were children."[3] The reason that Marcelline only remembers seeing her father's collection as a child might be that it met the same fate as the one of Nick Adams's father.

Ernest Hemingway's attitude towards his Grandfather Hall was revealed in a letter (written in 1920 to a friend) in which he discussed the skeletons in his family closet. In this letter, he began his paragraph with news that his grandfather had gambled away a fortune. He was probably referring to an incident which his sister wrote about in her book: ". . . and once, for a matter of a few hours, Mother told us, Abba had something called 'a corner in wheat' and was a potential millionaire. But in a short time he had lost it all, and, disappointed, returned to his more modest investments."[4] What Marcelline thought was a great feat of her grandfather's, her brother had interpreted as a disgrace.

While Grandfather Hall was born and educated in England, Grandfather Hemingway was from the East, born in East Plymouth, Connecticut. He was proud of his American heritage and traced his Hemingway ancestors back to the American Revolution. His printed biography in pamphlet form was distributed at his funeral in 1926. The entire contents of the pamphlet are here included, because they give not only the biography of Ernest Hemingway's grandfather, whom the writer resembled in appearance in his later years, but also an insight into the upper-middle-class, churchgoing background from which the writer sprung.

. . . . .

Anson Tyler Hemingway
August 26, 1844–October 7, 1926
ANSON T. HEMINGWAY

Death of Pioneer and Distinguished Citizen
Who Was Father of Large and Influential Family

The passing of Anson Tyler Hemingway on Thursday morning, Oct. 7 takes from Oak Park a citizen of outstanding character and influence. For more than fifty-eight years Mr. Hemingway was a citizen of this village, and during all of this time his influence was a helpful and constructive one in every department of life. He came to Oak Park from Wheaton college, which he entered after returning from honorable service in the 72nd Illinois infantry during the Civil War.

As a real estate man for many years he was influential in the development of the community and in bringing into it men who have become some if [sic] prominent citizens. For ten years he was general secretary of the Chicago Y.M.C.A. and enjoyed the friendly co-operation of Dwight L. Moody, who had been one of his predecessors in that office. Thru Mr. Hemingway's influence many of the association's most influential friends became interested, among them Jane L. Houghteling, John V. Farwell, and Cyrus H. McCormick. His administration meant the beginning of new and larger life in the association. Victor Lawson, for example, whose recent magnificent bequest of over $3,000,000 to the association has been one of the events of Chicgo's history, was induced to make his first gift and begin his interest in the association thru Mr. Hemingway.

During all the years since he came to Oak Park, Mr. Hemingway was an active and enthusiastic member of the First Congregational Church, serving as Sunday School superintendent, deacon, and finally becoming deacon emeritus, and by his friendly greeting bringing many people into relationship with the church. He maintained this interest up to the very end, not dwelling in the past days, but eagerly inquiring of the visitors to his sick-room as to the present work and future plans of the church, which he loved. The cause of temperance, the fellowship and the Grand Army men in Phil Sheridan post and the Borrowed Time Club, and every other civic enterprise, benefited by his interest. But beyond all institutions, the thing which endeared Mr. Hemingway to the community was his capacity for friendship. He was interested in persons more than in institutions. No one could meet him without carrying away a glow of friendship and a sense of his keen personal interest in their welfare. Even when confined to bed he continued to give away to the visitors who came, the very flowers and candy that had been sent to him.

Such a life as Mr. Hemingway's can be measured in part also by the way its influence has gone out thruout the world. All six of his children graduated from the Oak Park schools and went to Oberlin College and have made enviable places in the world. One is a highly esteemed doctor [Ernest's father], *one is a prominent business man, one an educational leader and another an honored missionary physician in charge of the Esther Barton Memorial hospital in Shansi, China. His son in China, Dr. Willoughby A. Hemingway, has not seen his father for nearly seven years. He is returning next year on his furlough. Another son, Alfred T. Hemingway, a leading businessman in Kansas City, died four years ago.*

Mr. Hemingway was especially happy in his married life. On August 27, 1869, Lieut. Anson T. Hemingway

ANSON TYLER HEMINGWAY

August 26, 1844
October 7, 1926

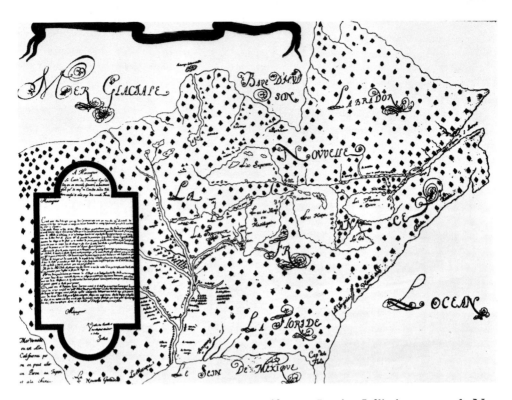

Above: Louis Jolliet's map of New France (1674) based on the Marquette-Jolliet voyage of 1673. Note the distortion of Lake Michigan, especially of the eastern shoreline. *Above, opposite page:* A turn-of-the-century map showing the railroad route the Hemingway family took. (The boat routes were for day lines, not for the boats the Hemingways took to Harbor Springs.) Walloon Lake was then called Bear Lake and Lake Charlevoix was called Pine Lake. *Lower, opposite page:* Railroad station at Bay View as it was when the Hemingway family first saw it.

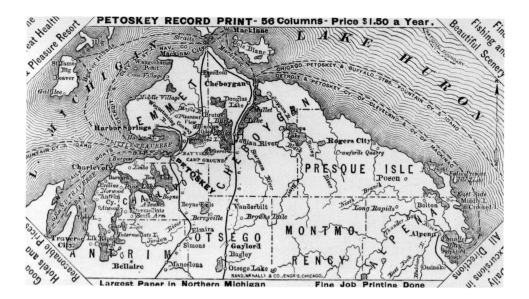

Above: An 1884 drawing of Harbor Springs and Harbor Point with Petoskey and Bay View in the distance. *Right:* A recent photograph of Harbor Springs (*photo: Virgil D. Haynes*).

Summer, 1917, near Horton Bay. *Left to right*, Madelaine "Sunny" Hemingway, Mrs. Hemingway (Ernest's mother), Mrs. Wesley Dilworth, Carol Hemingway.

Above: The Hemingway cottage. *Below:* Horton Bay. "The general store and post office with a high false front . . ."—"Up in Michigan"

and Miss Adelaide Edmunds were married and lived together for 54 years until her death in 1923. She shared his spirit of loyalty and devotion to the church and to all the higher interests of the community and no account of Mr. Hemingway's life is complete without a recognition of how large a part her influence was in both its joy and effective service.

Born in East Plymouth, Litchfield County, Conn., on August 26, 1844, Mr. Hemingway came to Chicago with his father, Allen Hemingway, in 1854, when the elder Hemingway was sent west from the New England states by Seth Thomas, the noted clockmaker.

Mr. Hemingway enlisted with the board of trade regiment of the Seventy-second Illinois Infantry, being promoted to the rank of lieutenant at the age of 19 years by President Lincoln.

Funeral services will be held at the family home 400 North Oak Park Avenue, at 2 o'clock this (Saturday) afternoon, conducted by his pastor, Rev. Albert W. Palmer, of the First Congregational Church.

The surviving members of the family are Mr. Frank B. Hines of Carbondale, Ill.; Dr. Willoughby A. Hemingway, of Taiku, Shansi, China; Dr. Clarence E. Hemingway [Ernest's father], George R. Hemingway, and Miss Grace A. Hemingway, all of Oak Park, twenty grandchildren and four great-grandchildren. A sister, Mrs. Alexander Smith of Norwood Park, Chicago, also survives.

. . . . .

Although Ernest Hemingway was not mentioned in the funeral pamphlet at the time of his grandfather's death, he had spent more time with his Grandfather Hemingway than with his Grandfather Hall, who had become just a childhood memory. In January, 1920, Hemingway wrote a letter mailed from Oak Park, in which he mentioned that his grandfather took him to lunch with Harry Lander. Hemingway noted that Mr. Lander was upset that Kaiser Wilhelm II had not been tried in the name of "Justice." Not only did his Grandfather Hemingway take his twenty-year-old grandson to lunch, but included him in the conversation about the Kaiser, who had fled to Holland and abdicated. The young Hemingway, who had participated and been wounded in the War, had earned the respect of the grandfather he respected.

Three High School Stories

While still living at home with his family in Oak Park, Hemingway wrote three short stories which were published in *Tabula*, the Oak Park High School's literary magazine. These stories show that he had formed the basis of his style, even as a junior in high school, and had chosen his subject matter of violence and manliness before his World War I experiences. These precocious stories, "Judgment of Manitou," "A Matter of Colour," and "Sepi Jingan," are well-written and distinctive enough to be identified as "Hemingway stories."

While only a junior at Oak Park High School, Hemingway wrote the story "Judgment of Manitou." A classmate who was editor on the *Tabula* during his and Hemingway's junior and senior years said, "Hemingway submitted a story or essay to the school magazine while I was on it." The editor was given the Hemingway manuscript by the magazine's faculty adviser, who received it from Miss Dixon, Hemingway's English teacher. The editor understood that "this essay or story about a hunting expedition was considered good enough by the teachers that it was to be printed whether it appealed to me or not."[1]

This story, published in the February, 1916, issue of *Tabula*, contains dialogue which is not forced and has brisk and lucid narrative. "Judgment of Manitou" deals with the raw material Hemingway lived with each summer and shows his early concern with nature and violence. The late Charles Fenton wrote that Hemingway treated this story of a vindictive trapper and the murder of his young associate in a manner reminiscent of Jack London. "Judgment of Manitou" is "a savage story tempered by irony."[2]

None of the grammar, punctuation, or spelling (except for a few typographical errors) was changed in the three following high school stories of Hemingway's. They appear here as they were first published for his Oak Park classmates.

. . . . .

JUDGMENT OF MANITOU
by Ernest Hemingway, '17

Dick Haywood buttoned the collar of his mackinaw up about his ears, took down his rifle from the deer horns above the fireplace of the cabin and pulled on his heavy fur mittens. "I'll go and run that line toward Loon River, Pierre", he said. "Holy quill pigs, but it's cold." He glanced at the thermometer. "Forty-two below! Well, so long, Pierre." Pierre merely grunted, as, twisting on his snowshoes, Dick started out over the crust with the swinging snowshoe stride of the traveler of the barren grounds.

In the doorway of the cabin Pierre stood looking after Dick as he swung along. He grinned evilly to himself, "De tief will tink it a blame sight cooler when he swingin by one leg in the air like Wah-boy, the rabbit; he would steal my money, would he!" Pierre slammed the heavy door shut, threw some wood on the fire and crawled into his bunk.

At [As] Dick Haywood strode along he talked to himself as to the travellers of the "silent places." "Wonder why Pierre is so grouchy just because he lost that money? Bet he just misplaced it somewhere. All he does now is to grunt like a surly pig and every once in a while I catch him leering at me behind my back. If he thinks I stole his money why don't he say so and have it out with me! Why, he used to be so cheerful and jolly; when we agreed at Missainabal to be partners and trap up here in the Ungave district, I thought he'd be a jolly good companion, but now he hasn't spoken to me for the last week, except to grunt or swear in that Cree lingo."

It was a cold day, but it was the dry, invigorating cold of the northland and Dick enjoyed the crisp air. He was a good traveller on snowshoes and rapidly covered the first five miles of the trap line, but somehow he felt that something was following him and he glanced around several times only to be disappointed each time. "I guess it's only the kootzie-ootzie," he muttered to himself, for in the North whenever men do not understand a thing they blame it on the "little bad god of the Cree." Suddenly, as Dick entered a growth of spruce, he was jerked off his feet, high into the air. When his head had cleared from the bang it had received by striking the icy crust, he saw that he was suspended in the air by a rope which was attached to a spruce tree, which had been bent over to form the spring for a snare, such as is used to capture rabbits. His fingers barely touched the crust, and as he struggled and the cord grew tighter on his led [leg] he saw what he had sensed to be following him. Slowly out of the woods trotted a band of gaunt, white, hungry timber wolves, and squatted on their haunches in a circle round him.

Back in the cabin Pierre as he lay in his bunk was awakened by a gnawing sound overhead, and idly looking up at the rafter he saw a red squirrel busily gnawing away at the leather of his lost wallet. He thought of the trap he had set for Dick, and springing from his bunk he seized his rifle, and coatless and gloveless ran madly out along the trail. After a gasping, breathless, choking run he came upon the spruce grove. Two ravens left off picking at the shapeless something that had once been Dick Haywood, and flapped lazily into a neighboring spruce. All over the bloody snow were the tracks of My-in-gau, the timber wolf.

As he took a step forward Pierre felt the clanking grip of the toother bear trap, that Dick had come to tend, close on his feet. He fell forward, and as he lay on the snow he said; "It is the judgement of Manitou; I will save My-in-gau, the wolf, the trouble."

And he reached for the rifle.

•　•　•　•　•

The young writer of "Judgment of Manitou" in about seven hundred words was able to create suspense, develop the reader's interest in his characters, and to spring a surprise ending. Hemingway not only sustained the pace of the story, but he showed signs of his later choice of subject matter. Two rough men on the frontier, probably northern Canada (the Missinaibi River is in East Central Ontario while the Ungava Region is east of Hudson Bay), have a conflict which is resolved in a double death: one murder and one suicide.

Since much of the conflict between the trapper and his associate was framed in the mysticism of Indian folklore, the information Hemingway was writing about or elaborating on must have been gathered from his Indian friends. The word "Manitou" is the Ottawa Indian word for "God"; a confusing point, since the Indians whom Hemingway wrote about in his short stories were Ojibwas.

An Ottawa Indian woman, who runs the Chief Blackbird Museum in Harbor Springs, helped to clear the point when she said that the Chippewas and Ojibwas are the same tribe. She also added, "Ojibwa is the Indian name. Chippewa is the white man's mispronunciation of it." She said that the Ottawa, Potawatami, and Chippewa Indians were all Algonquins, and that they had many similarities in their languages. She also offered the information that her generation (which would be Hemingway's) knew the Indian language and spoke it. The word "Manitou" could also have been used by the Ojibwa tribe, as well as by the Ottawas. The Ojibwas whom Hemingway knew must have formed a small settlement away from the old Ojibwa Indian nation which was on the Lake Huron, not the Lake Michigan, side of the state. Hemingway's use of the Indian word, "Ojibway" (an alternate spelling which Hemingway used), instead of the "white man's" word, "Chippewa," is further evidence that his association with the Indians was personal and direct.

. . . . .

"A Matter of Colour," published in the April, 1916, issue of the *Tabula* during Hemingway's junior year, is more an anecdote than a short story and does not have the tension, setting, or drama of Hemingway's other two stories included in this chapter. "A Matter of Colour" is a story that should be read aloud, for the accents, slang, and punchline make it a narrative "story-joke."

. . . . .

A MATTER OF COLOUR
by Ernest Hemingway

"What, you never heard the story about Joe Gan's first fight?" said old Bob Armstrong, as he tugged at one of his gloves.

"Well, son, that kid I was just giving the lesson to reminded me of the Big Swede that gummed the best frame-up we ever almost pulled off.

"The yarn's a classic now; but I'll give it to you just as it happened.

"Along back in 1902 I was managing a sort of a new lightweight by the name of Montana Dan Morgan. Well, this Dan person was one of those rough and ready lads, game and all that, but with no footwork, but with a kick like a mule in his right fin, but with a weak left that wouldn't dent melted butter. I'd gotten along pretty well with the bird, and we'd collected sundry shekels fighting dockwallopers and stevedores and preliminary boys out at the old Olympic club.

"Dan was getting to be quite a sizable scrapper, and by using his strong right mitt and stalling along, he managed to achieve quite a reputation. So I matched the lad with Jim O'Rourke, the old trial horse, and the boy managed to hang one on Jim's jaw that was good for the ten-second anesthetic.

"So when Pete McCarthy came around one day and said he had an amateur that wanted to break in, and would I sign Dan up with him for twenty rounds out at Vernon, I fell for it strong. Joe Gans, Pete said, was the amateur's name, and I'd never heard of him at that time.

"I thought that it was kind of strange when Pete came around with a contract that had a $500 forfeit clause in it for non-appearance, but we intended to appear all right, so I signed up.

"Well, we didn't train much for the scrap, and two days before it was to come off, Dan comes up to me and says: "Bob, take a look at this hand.'

"He stuck out his right mauler, and there, just above the wrist, was a lump like a pigeon egg.

" 'Holy smokes! Danny, where did you get that?'

" 'The bag busted loose while I was punchin' it,' says Danny, 'and me right banged into the framework.'

" 'Well, you've done it now,' I yelped. 'There's that 500 iron men in the forfeit, and I've put down everything I've got on you to win by K.O.'

" 'It can't be helped,' says Dan. 'That bag wasn't fastened proper; I'll fight anyway.'

" 'Yes, you will, with that left hand of yours, that couldn't punch a ripple in a bowl of soup.'

" 'Bob,' says Danny, 'I've got a scheme. You know the way the ring is out there at the Olympic? Up on the stage with that old cloth drop curtain in back? Well, in the first round, before they find out about this bad flipper of mine, I'll rush the smoke up against the curtain (you know Joe Gans was a "pusson of color") and you have somebody back there with a baseball bat, and swat him on the head from behind the curtain.'

"Say! I could have thrown a fit. It was so blame simple. We just couldn't lose, you see. It comes off so quick nobody gets wise. Then we collects and beats it!

"So I goes out and pawns my watch to put another twenty down on Dan to win by a knockout. Then we went out to Vernon and I hired a big husky Swede to do the slapstick act.

"The day of the fight dawned bright and clear, as the sporting writers say, only it was foggy. I installed the husky Swede back of the old drop curtain just behind the ropes.

You see, I had every cent we had down on Dan, about 600 round ones and the 500 in the forfeit. A couple of ham and egg fighters mauled each other in the prelims, and then the bell rings for our show.

"I tied Dan's gloves on, gives him a chew of gum and my blessing, and he climbs over the ropes into the squared circle. This Joe Gans, he's champion now, had quite a big following among the Oakland gang, and so we had no very great trouble getting out [*our*] money covered. Joe's black, you know, and the Swede behind the scenes had his instructions: 'Just as soon as the white man backs the black man up against the ropes, you swing on the black man's head with the bat from behind the curtain.'

"Well, the gong clangs and Dan rushes the smoke up against the ropes, according to instructions.

"Nothing doing from behind the curtain! I motioned wildly at the Swede looking out through the peephole.

"Then Joe Gans rushes Dan up against the ropes. Whunk! comes a crack and Dan drops like a poled over ox.

"Holy smoke! The Swede had hit the wrong man! All our kale was gone! I climbed into the ring, grabbed Dan and dragged him into the dressing room by the feet. There wasn't any need for the referee to count ten; he might have counted 300.

"There was the Swede.

"I lit into him: 'You miserable apology for a low-grade imbecile! You evidence of God's carelessness! Why in the name of the Prophet did you hit the white man instead of the black man?'

" 'Mister Armstrong,' he says, 'you no should talk at me like that—I bane color blind!' "

.   .   .   .   .

During his senior year, 1916–17, when most of the urge to write was being satisfied by his work for the school newspaper, Hemingway did find time to produce "Sepi Jingan," included in the November, 1916 issue of the *Tabula*. Largely dialogue and with a Michigan background, this was a tale of violence and revenge told by an Ojibwa Indian.

Hemingway, in his previous high school writing for the newspaper, had used satire as well as straight reporting. In the case of "Judgment of Manitou," he had created a plot from either secondary sources or his imagination, but in "Sepi Jingan" he wrote about a setting he was familiar with, about an Indian he knew personally, and recounted a story which the Indian might have told him. In this more sophisticated story, Hemingway had the same clarity of narrative and certainty of style that he always had when he knew the subject from first-hand experience and had not created it out of his imagination.

.   .   .   .   .

SEPI JINGAN
by Ernest Hemingway, '17

" 'Velvets' like red hot pepper; 'P.A.' like cornsilk. Give me a package of 'Peerless.' "

Billy Tabeshaw, long, lean, copper-colored, hamfaced and Ojibway, spun a Canadian quarter onto the counter of the little north-woods country store and stood waiting for the clerk to get his change from the till under the notion counter.

"Hey, you robber!" yelled the clerk. "Come back here!"

We all had a glimpse of a big, wolfish-looking, husky dog vanishing through the door with a string of frankfurter sausages bobbing, snake-like, behind him.

"Darn that blasted cur! Them sausages are on you, Bill."

"Don't cuss the dog. I'll stand for the meat. What's it set me back?"

"Just twenty-nine cents, Bill. There was three pounds of 'em at ten cents, but I et one of 'em myself."

"Here's thirty cents. Go buy yourself a picture post-card."

Bill's dusky face cracked across in a white-toothed grin. He put his package of tobacco under his arm and slouched out of the store. At the door he crooked a finger at me and I followed him out into the cool twilight of the summer evening.

At the far end of the wide porch three pipes glowed in the dusk.

"Ish," said Bill, "they're smoking 'Stag!' It smells like dried apricots. Me for 'Peerless.' "

Bill is not the redskin of the popular magazine. He never says "ugh." I have yet to hear him grunt or speak of the Great White Father at Washington. His chief interests are the various brands of tobacco and his big dog, "Sepi Jingan."

We strolled off down the road. A little way ahead, through the gathering darkness, we could see a blurred figure. A whiff of smoke reached Bill's nostrils. "Gol, that guy is smoking 'Giant'! No, it's 'Honest Scrap'! Just like burnt rubber hose. Me for 'Peerless.' "

The edge of the full moon showed above the hill to the east. To our right was a grassy bank. "Let's sit down," Bill said. "Did I ever tell you about Sepi Jingan?"

"Like to hear it," I replied.

"You remember Paul Black Bird?"

"The new fellow who got drunk last fourth of July and went to sleep on the Pere Marquette tracks?"

"Yes. He was a bad Indian. Up on the upper peninsula he couldn't get drunk. He used to drink all day—everything. But he couldn't get drunk. Then he would go crazy; but he wasn't drunk. He was crazy because he couldn't get drunk.

"Paul was Jack-fishing (spearing fish illegally) over on Witch Lake up on the upper, and John Brandar, who was game warden, went over to pinch him. John always did a job like that alone: so next day, when he didn't show up, his wife sent me over to look for him. I found him, all right. He was lying at the end of the portage, all spread out, face down and a pike-pile stuck through his back.

"They raised a big fuss and the sheriff hunted all over for Paul; but there never was a white man yet could catch an Indian in the Indian's own country.

"But with me, it was quite different. You see, John Brandar was my cousin.

"I took Sepi, who was just a pup then, and we trailed him (that was two years ago). We trailed him to the Soo, lost the trail, picked it up at Garden River, in Ontario; followed him along the north shore to Michipicoten; and then he went up to Missainabie and 'way up to Moose Factory. We were always just behind him, but we never could catch up. He doubled back by the Abittibi and finally thought he'd ditched us. He came down to this country from Mackinaw.

"We trailed him, though, but lost the scent and just happened to hit this place. We didn't know he was here, but he had us spotted.

"Last fourth of July I was walking by the P.M. tracks with Sepi when something hit me alongside the head and everything went black. ·

"When I came to, there was Paul Black Bird standing over me with a pike-pole and grinning at me!

" 'Well,' he smiled, 'you have caught up with me; ain't you glad to see me?'

"There was when he made a mistake. He should have killed me then and everything would have been all right for him. He would have, if he had been either drunk or sober, but had been drinking and was crazy. That was what saved me.

"He kept prodding me with the pike-pole and kidding me. 'Where's your dog, dog man? You and he have followed me. I will kill you both and then slide you onto the rails.'

"All the time I kept wondering where Sepi was. Finally I saw him. He was crawling with his belly on the earth toward Black Bird. Nearer and nearer he crawled and I prayed that Paul wouldn't see him.

"Paul sat there, cussing and pricking me with the long pike-pole. Sepi crawled closer and closer. I watched him out of the tail of my eye while I looked at Paul.

"Suddenly Sepi sprang like a shaggy thunderbolt. With a side snap of his head, his long, wolf jaws caught the throat.

"It was really a very neat job, considering. The Pere Marquette Resort Limited removed all the traces. So, you see, when you said that Paul Black Bird was drunk and lay down on the Pere Marquette tracks you weren't quite right. That Indian couldn't get drunk. He only got crazy on drink.

"That's why you and me are sittin' here, lookin' at the moon, and my debts are paid and I let Sepi steal sausages at Hauley's store.

"Funny, ain't it?

"You take my advice and stay off that 'Tuxedo'—'Peerless' is the only tobacco.

"Come on, Sepi."

. . . . .

"Sepi Jingan," is the most mature of Hemingway's high school stories. In it the young writer drew directly from the Michigan countryside and people he knew. "Hauley's store" is probably the false-front country store in the town of Horton Bay. "Billy Tabeshaw" appears again as a fictional character in the stories "The Doctor and the Doctor's Wife" and "Ten Indians." But Billy Tabeshaw was also the name of a flesh-and-blood Indian who lived in the Indian camp near the Hemingway cottage. Hemingway describes Billy Tabeshaw as being long and lean in "Sepi Jingan." However, he later described him in "The Doctor and the Doctor's Wife" as being fat, and the residents of Walloon Lake remember Billy as being fat, not long and lean.

Although the story which Billy tells the summer resident in "Sepi Jingan" may have been fictional (a fictional story within a fictional story), the possibility exists that it actually could have happened. The real Billy Tabeshaw could have tracked an Indian named Paul Black Bird for two years, and his dog, Sepi Jingan, might have killed a man.

Hemingway himself probably did not know an Indian by the name of Paul Black Bird, but he might have fictionalized an Indian he did know and used the historic Indian name of "Blackbird," the name of the famous Ottawa chief for whom the museum in Harbor Springs was named.

An elderly neighbor of the Hemingways' remembered several Indians, whom he had known personally and whom Ernest probably also had known, who had met death when they had fallen asleep on the railroad tracks. The tracks of the Pere Marquette railroad ran parallel to the side of Walloon Lake where the Hemingway cottage stands. This same neighbor said that the father of Tommy Mitchell, an Indian who was a friend of Ernest's and who was fictionalized in "The Light of the World," lived in

Petoskey. One night Tommy Mitchell's father was drunk; he fell asleep on the railroad tracks and was killed instantly when run over by a train. Another Indian family from near Walloon Lake, the Quazicums, had four boys, and of these four only one was not run over by a train while drunk. Hemingway undoubtedly heard about these Indians and maybe even knew them when he was a boy.

The reference in "Sepi Jingan" to the Upper Peninsula means the upper part of Michigan which is beyond the Straits of Mackinac. This allusion plus the one about the Pere Marquette tracks definitely sets the scene of this story near the Hemingway summer home on Walloon Lake.

. . . . .

Of these three previously unpublished stories, "Sepi Jingan" seems to foreshadow Hemingway's later work most accurately. The humor in "Sepi Jingan" comes from the more subtle contrasts of the Indian's character; while in "A Matter of Colour" the sophomoric humor is still broad and like his later newspaper writing for the Toronto *Star Weekly*. The involved plot and surprise ending of "Judgment of Manitou" foreshadow such later stories as "The Snows of Kilimanjaro," while the hidden recesses of character and the theme that people are not what they seem to be link "Sepi Jingan" with such later stories as "The Sea Change" and "The Short Happy Life of Francis Macomber."

Not one to be attracted by the easy sentimentalism of the writing in 1916–17, Hemingway had already chosen his subject matter of rough men pitted against nature and their own characters, of murderers—Indian, in this case— explaining life's rules to the young initiate, and of the life in and about the prize ring. He would later expand these themes but not change his basic thesis.

In these three high school stories Hemingway first exhibited his concern with death, often violent death. He even used the clipped dialogue, the fast-paced action, and the diamond-hard brilliance of style which became his trademarks. Although Hemingway wrote these stories when he was only seventeen and eighteen, they all bear his unmistakable stamp.

The Indian Camp

If you walk east from the Hemingway cottage along Lake
Grove Drive, turn north on Resort Pike for a few hundred
yards, and then walk east again on Indian Garden Road,
you will come to the site of the former Ojibwa Indian
camp. Several years ago, one deserted shack still remained.
Sunlight filtered between the cracks in the wall, and the
potbellied stove, rusted and covered with debris, still stood
in the largest of the small rooms. Outside, a yellow daisy
grew in the tangled weeds of what was once a garden.

As a boy, Ernest Hemingway spent his summers near
the Indian camp, and he came to know its inhabitants. A
lumber mill then stood behind the cluster of shanties
where the Indians lived, worked as barkpeelers, and took
their meals communally. Hemingway played, hunted, and
fished with the Indian children and also grew to know
their parents. Because of their proximity, many of the
summer residents knew all of the Indian families who lived
by the trail to the lumber camp, which was behind the old
Echo Beach Hotel. When Hemingway was a child, a full
day was needed to go to Petoskey by horse and wagon for
supplies or medical emergencies. When anyone was ill or
injured in the community of lumbermen, summer residents, farmers, and Indian barkpeelers living by the shores
of Walloon Lake, Doctor Hemingway was called to treat
the patient.

The story "Indian Camp" has a setting resembling the Indian camp behind the Hemingway cottage. This story is important from both a literary and biographical point of view because it was the first published "Nick Adams" story. In this short story Nick is a child of about eight or nine years. "Indian Camp" first appeared in the Paris edition of *in our time*, a little book which William Bird printed on handmade Rives paper in an edition of 170 copies on a hand press in the downstairs part of the *transatlantic review* office. The *transatlantic review* was a small magazine which originated in Paris in January, 1924, and was edited by Ford Madox Ford. *in our time* was finally published in the spring of 1924, after a series of delays. Bird was fussy about the design of the boards (a montage of headlines from the world press) and about the appearance of the woodcut, made from a portrait of Hemingway by his friend Henry Strater, which was used as a frontispiece. Another cause of delay was the binder, who kept the sheets for two months.

A review of the little thirty-two-page book was written in time to meet the March first deadline for the April issue of the *transatlantic review*. What struck that reviewer (who signed only his initials, M.R.) most forcibly was the brevity of the stories. The author seized, the review said, those "moments when life is condensed and cleancut and significant, presenting them in minute narratives that eliminate every useless word. Each tale is much longer than the measure of its lines."[1] The April *transatlantic* also contained this same story, "Indian Camp," entitled "Work in Progress." Along with two of the stories from the Robert McAlmon edition of *Three Stories and Ten Poems*, published in Paris in the summer of 1923, "Indian Camp" formed the nucleus around which Hemingway was building his own work in progress. The question also arises at this point in his career as to whether Hemingway intended "Indian Camp" to be a chapter in a novel with Nick Adams as its possible main character.

In "Indian Camp" Nick's father, a doctor, delivers an Indian woman of a baby by Caesarean section with a jackknife and without anesthetic. The woman's invalid husband lies in a bunk above his screaming wife. Nick holds a basin for his father while a man and three women hold the mother until the child is successfully born. When the Caesarean is over, the doctor looks in the upper bunk and discovers that the husband, who has been lying there through two days of screaming, had fatally cut his throat with a razor.

"Indian Camp" is a story of Nick's initiation to pain and to the violence of birth and death. The story is written objectively and completely without comment. The book of short stories, *In Our Time* (in the American edition, published by Boni and Liveright, the title was conventionally capitalized), is nearly a novel about Nick Adams, so closely related are the stories in which he appears. Hemingway began this first story about Nick by using a pattern of contacts with evil and violence that he developed in the rest of the stories until he had built what is actually a plot; and "Indian Camp," as part of this plot, is Nick's story, not the doctor's or the Indians'.

"Indian Camp" clearly takes place on Walloon Lake at the Indian camp behind the Hemingway cottage. In the first sentence the scene is set at the lakeshore, where two Indians are waiting with rowboats. Nick and his father get into one rowboat, which one of the Indians rows, while "Uncle George" sits in the stern of the "camp rowboat," rowed by another Indian.

The "camp rowboat" was probably owned by the lumber camp. The forest was thick in 1907 (the approximate date for the story) and the faster mode of travel was by water. Although another lumber mill was on the opposite side of the lake, west of Wildwood harbor, most of the residents who were living near the Hemingway cottage in 1907 only remembered Indians living and working at the nearby camp, while regular lumberjacks were employed at the one on the other side of the lake from the Hemingway cottage.

When Mrs. George Depew, a neighbor of the Hemingways', described the Indian camp as it was in Ernest's day, she said, "it was off Resort Pike road and all of the Indians lived and worked at the lumber camp which was in operation then. These particular Indians were bark-peelers and when the lumber camp stopped operating, they all moved away. They lived in shanties around the lumber camp and all ate together in one shanty." Mrs. Depew used the word "shanty" when referring to the Indians' ramshackle homes as did Hemingway in this story.

The "Uncle George" mentioned in this story seems to be taken directly from Hemingway's life. George Hemingway was Doctor Hemingway's brother who lived in Boyne City. He had a reputation for being a good businessman and owned a large plot of ground near the Ironton Ferry where he had his tree nursery. Several people in Boyne City who knew George Hemingway said that he was a calm, sedate man. One woman said that "when my father died, George gave my mother some flowers free for my father's funeral." But Mrs. Wesley Dilworth said, "When George read that story, 'Indian Camp,' he just shook his head and said 'not a word of it is true.' "

Hemingway's sister Sunny took the same attitude as her Uncle George, for she said:

> *Now, here's another thing. Our dad was ministering time and time again to the Indians that lived in the lumber camp near us. Mostly it was firewater trouble, juniper-berry trouble, pneumonia, etc. I'd swear there was never a Caesarian performed as per Ernie's story where you tell of his seeing such violence in his youth.*

The guy is a story-teller and he did not live every moment he has the imagination to write about. People forever read into any good fellow's works meanings that are not anything but putrid in reality.[2]

It is possible that Hemingway's sister, five years his junior, would not have been told of the Indian camp experience, if it actually happened.

Leicester Hemingway, remembering his father, the Indian camp, and his brother Ernest, wrote:

Even at Windemere, Father spent a certain amount of time practicing medicine. He was the only doctor on the lake then. And there was an Ojibway Indian camp at the abandoned sawmill less than two miles away. These Indians were the poor of the area, owning no land and seldom holding jobs for long since all the big timber had been logged out. They had regular emergencies—stabbings, broken bones, serious infections, Ernest often went with Father on these calls. Not only did he admire many of the Ojibways, he learned a lot about emergency medicine under primitive conditions.[3]

Although Leicester was not born until Ernest was fifteen years old, he had visited the Indian camp himself. Both his father and his brother might have told him about their experiences as he grew up.

It is possible that George Hemingway did not accompany Ernest and his father when Doctor Hemingway performed a Caesarean. But "Uncle George" was enough like George Hemingway, so that his neighbors could identify him and ask him about this story. Hemingway's younger sister, Sunny, said that Hemingway did not accompany his father on such a trip, but she states that her father was a doctor, as in the story, and knew the Indians well enough to minister to them.

Two of the residents of Walloon Lake in 1907, John McConnell and Joseph Bacon, who knew both the Hemingways and the Indians, reminisced about the "old days." John McConnell, a distinguished-looking man whose family owned the old Echo Beach Hotel, now lives near the site where the hotel stood by Indian Garden Road.

McConnel described the Indian camp, which was behind the hotel, and the Indians who lived there: "The Indians who lived at the lumber camp would peel the bark and cut up the wood the loggers would bring into the camp. They would cut it into thirty-three-inch planks. They would then haul the lumber on sleighs over the ice on the lake in the winter to Boyne City. A chemical plant was in Boyne City for the rest of the 'stuff.' Some of the Indians stayed in the lumber camp after the lumbermen left, living in old shanties and tents. Most of them left though before World War I, when the trees were all cut down. They were Chippewas, close to the Ottawa tribe, very little difference, and spoke Indian among themselves."

John McConnell liked Doctor Hemingway and thought that he was "the pick of the bunch." According to McConnell, the Hemingways stayed at the Echo Beach Hotel for two or three summers before they built their own cottage. "Doc Hemingway would take care of anyone who was sick at the hotel," remembered McConnell, "and also went back into the lumber camp to take care of the Indians. He took Ernie along sometimes."

Joseph Bacon, who is probably the fictional "Joe Garner" in the story "Ten Indians," was ninety years old when he was interviewed in 1960. Tall, with a shock of white hair, Joseph Bacon at that age was still a rugged and handsome man; he had the healthy look of a successful farmer who has spent much of his life out of doors. In 1960 he lived in a small house in the hills outside of

Petoskey where he kept many mementos of the Hemingway family.

He knew not only the Hemingways, but all of the Indians who lived at the lumber camp. He confirmed the fact that the lumber camp was across the road from his farm, and that all of the Indians lived in "shanties over there." He also remembered that Doctor Hemingway treated the Indians and delivered babies in people's houses. Doctor Hemingway had delivered the child of Joseph Bacon's eldest sister, who lived two or three miles away from the Hemingway cottage.

In the story "Indian Camp," Hemingway writes that the doctor's party and the Indians beached their boats and then walked to the Indian camp. The description of the route taken by the three men and the boy following the young Indian—up from the beach through a meadow, into the woods, then to a trail that led to the logging road that ran back into the hills, and finally to the Indian camp—is totally recognizable. Indian Garden Road today follows the old logging road, and the meadow was part of the Bacon farm. When Hemingway's characters came around a bend in the road, they saw "the lights of the shanties where the Indian barkpeelers lived . . . in the shanty nearest the road there was a light in the window."[4] Only one building remained in 1960 (it has since been torn down) from the lumber camp buildings and the shanties around them. The remaining shanty was the one "nearest the road," and could be viewed first from a bend in the road leading to the Hemingway cottage. This shanty belonged to an Indian family named Gilbert who had three children. John McConnell did not remember a Caesarian or a suicide in that family, but he thought that it might be possible. At the end of the story, when Nick and his father are rowing back to their own place, Hemingway describes the sun coming up over the hills and a jumping bass which made a circle in the water.

Separating fact from fiction is more difficult in "Indian Camp" than in other of Hemingway's Michigan stories, but several facts emerge. An Indian camp did exist near the Hemingway cottage, and Doctor Hemingway was the doctor who tended the Indian families. Young Ernest Hemingway often accompanied his father on these trips. The physical description of the lake, road, land, and the Indian shanty are accurate renditions of real places, and the route taken in the story can be traced today. The "doctor-father" and "Uncle George" both resemble their real-life counterparts.

Whether the young boy Ernest Hemingway witnessed a Caesarian and a suicide in an Indian shanty cannot now be determined. It is probable that Hemingway, then writing in Paris, added a Caesarian and suicide to a childhood memory of a trip with his father and uncle to treat a less dramatic Indian ailment.

The relationship between the father and his son in this story is shown subtly. When Nick asks his father to give the Indian woman something to make her stop screaming, his father answers that he does not hear the screams, because they are not important. The sentence following the doctor's statement is a one-sentence paragraph: "The husband in the upper bunk rolled over against the wall."[5] The boy was right—at the end of the story the reader knows that the screams were important. If the woman had not shown her suffering through the screams, the husband probably would not have committed suicide. After the doctor finds out that the husband has killed himself, he regrets having brought his son along and apologizes to him.

But it is too late for apologies; the son has seen everything. As they row back in the boat, Nick has a conversation with his father about the pain of childbirth, suicide, the difference between male and female suicides, and death itself. As a young boy, Nick found out that women suffer bringing life into the world, but they rarely kill themselves. Men, on the other hand, are more likely to kill themselves when they cannot stand things. Since Nick and his father are men, Nick wants to know how dying feels. The story ends optimistically with the description of the lake scene and Nick's childish thought that he will never die.

In Hemingway's literary life those few lines of "Indian Camp" also have later echoes. In *A Farewell to Arms* the heroine dies in childbirth and in *For Whom the Bell Tolls* Robert Jordon's father had committed suicide. While Hemingway was in Paris, he wrote a poem about suicides, "Montparnasse," which appeared in *Three Stories and Ten Poems*, at approximately the same time that he wrote this story.

The thought of suicide seized the imagination of the young Hemingway and plagued him throughout his life. He thought of it first when he was wounded in 1919, later felt ambiguous about his father's suicide, and made his final decision about it on July 2, 1961.

Doctor and Mrs. Hemingway

According to the late biographer Charles Fenton, Ernest Hemingway once "declared that the best training for a writer was an unhappy boyhood."[1] Out of this training came two of his most autobiographical stories; both are about his parents. "The Doctor and the Doctor's Wife" appeared in the *transatlantic review* in December, 1924, and then in *In Our Time* on October 5, 1925. "Fathers and Sons" was published eight years later in *Winner Take Nothing* (October 27, 1933).

An incident happened to Doctor Hemingway in 1912, when Ernest was thirteen, which was the inspiration for "The Doctor and the Doctor's Wife." It is probably safe to assume that the age of Nick Adams in the story is also about thirteen. Within the context of the story, "Fathers and Sons," Nicholas Adams (Hemingway used the full name "Nicholas," instead of the nickname "Nick," in this story, probably to indicate the maturity of his character) describes himself as being thirty-eight years old.

"The Doctor and the Doctor's Wife" is less violent than the preceding Michigan stories, but no less scarring is its psychological impact on the young observer. Here Nick Adams is not involved with the birth and death of strangers, but with the emotional crosscurrents within his own family. For perhaps the first time, the disturbing relationship and attitudes of his parents are revealed to him.

"The Doctor and the Doctor's Wife" is about a work-man who picks a fight with Doctor Adams in order to avoid paying a large bill he owes for treatment of his wife. The doctor refuses to fight, and Nick's mother, who is a Christian Scientist and will not believe that a man would do what the workman has just done, quotes from the Bible. The father tells Nick that his mother wants him, but Nick ignores her request, because he cannot accept her naïve refusal to admit evil, and chooses instead to go squirrel shooting with his father.

Hemingway once said the following about his fictional characters: "Some come from real life. Mostly you invent people from a knowledge and understanding and experience of people."[2] The characters of "The Doctor and the Doctor's Wife" have come from real life. Carlos Baker substantiated this fact when he wrote:

> The Doctor and the Doctor's Wife is virtually a playback between Dr. Hemingway and a halfbreed Indian sawyer on the shore of Walloon Lake in the summer of 1912, with the youthful Ernest Hemingway as an interested onlooker. This is proved by a letter from his father to Ernest, written some 13 years after the event.[3]

Leicester Hemingway included in his book the information contained in a letter written on March 20, 1925, by Ernest Hemingway to his father, probably in reply to the letter mentioned by Carlos Baker.

> He [Ernest] said he was glad Father had liked the Doctor story ["The Doctor and the Doctor's Wife"] and that he had used the real names of Dick Bolton and Billy Tabeshaw because he doubted they would have access to a copy of the Transatlantic Review.[4]

Hemingway opened his story by writing about Dick Boulton, who came from the Indian camp to cut logs for

Nick's father and who brought along his son Eddy and another Indian named Billy Tabeshaw. (Billy Tabeshaw was also a character in the high school story "Sepi Jingan.") John McConnell, whose description of the Indian camp is in the preceding chapter, said that "there was a Billy Tabeshaw and a Billy Mitchell. Old man Tabeshaw lived over near Horton Bay. Dick Boulton was the father of Eddy and Prudence." (Prudence appeared later in "Ten Indians" and "Fathers and Sons.") "Dick was a white man but lived in the camp with a squaw called 'Annie.'" McConnell's recollection reinforces the information contained in Leicester Hemingway's book. Joseph Bacon also remembered the Indians Hemingway wrote about and said, "Billy Tabeshaw is now dead, but he was nice, sorta short, and stout. Dick Boulton was half French and half Indian."

Next in "The Doctor and the Doctor's Wife" there is a description of the Indians as they go down to the lake where they are supposed to saw up some logs for Doctor Adams. In the story the logs had been lost from the log booms which were towed down the lake to the mill by the steamer "Magic."

A steamer named the "Magic" actually had plied back and forth on Walloon Lake, according to old residents, and it sometimes towed logs when not carrying passengers. A sawmill stood on the side of Walloon Lake opposite the Hemingway cottage, several miles west of Wildwood Harbor. The superintendent and other executives of the mill lived in cabins along the shore, and the millhands lived in bunkhouses behind the mill. In the forests bordering the lake, the trees were cut, trimmed, and loaded onto log booms to be drawn to the mill. Steam-driven tugs, the "Magic" and her sister ships, would drag the log booms down the lake. Sometimes, when the wind kicked up, a boom would get loose with a load, and the lumbermen would be unable to retrieve it. Later, a crew of the

"Magic" would row along the shoreline searching for the escaped logs. When they found them, they would drive ringed spikes in their ends and tow them away.

The next paragraph of "The Doctor and the Doctor's Wife" gives a description of Dick Boulton as he cuts the logs. Dick walks around past the cottage down to the lake and puts three axes on the dock. Dick is described in the story as a half-breed whom many of the farmers around the lake thought to be a white man. Hemingway characterizes him as a lazy man, but a good worker when he worked. In the story, Dick bites off a "chew" from a plug of tobacco and speaks in Ojibwa to the Indians.

Dick then accuses Doctor Adams of stealing the logs, and the doctor challenges him to fight:

> *Dick Boulton looked at the doctor. Dick was a big man. He knew how big a man he was. He liked to get into fights. The doctor chewed the beard on his lower lip and looked at Dick Boulton. Then he turned away and walked up the hill to the cottage.*[5]

From the neighbors' descriptions of the real Dick Boulton, it is easy to visualize this large, aggressive man described in the above quotation pitted against Doctor Hemingway, the pacifist with a beard on his lower lip.

The actions of Billy Tabeshaw in the next paragraph contrast to those of Dick Boulton. Billy does not laugh about the cowardice Doctor Adams shows when Dick makes a remark in Ojibwa, and when Dick leaves the gate open as they depart, Billy goes back to fasten it. In the story Hemingway described Billy as not understanding English, although he was sweating while the row was going on, and being fat with only a few hairs of moustache, like a Chinaman.

Here is a glimpse of the real Billy Tabeshaw in a story related by Joseph Bacon: "The people from the lumber company wanted me to keep an eye on the Indians, be-

cause they would all make dandelion wine and get drunk
and cause trouble. One night Billy Tabeshaw came over
to my farmhouse. He said that they were all drunk and
wanted to kill him. He spent the night, and the Indians
stayed away. Next morning he went back to the camp,
but they had all sobered up and none of them bothered
Billy."

The remaining action in the story deals with the relationship between the doctor and his wife, who might be
Ernest Hemingway's own parents, except for a few details. Mrs. Adams is a Christian Scientist while Mrs. Hemingway was not. (Her daughter Marcelline, when asked
whether her mother was a Christian Scientist, said:
"Heavens no, how could she be, married to a doctor?")
When Hemingway wrote this story, he probably made the
doctor's wife a Christian Scientist to heighten the already
apparent differences between Doctor and Mrs. Adams.
Doctor and Mrs. Hemingway were members of the Congregational Church. Mrs. Hemingway was baptized an
Episcopalian, but she became a Congregationalist when she
married Doctor Hemingway in the First Congregational
Church in Oak Park on October 1, 1896.

When Mrs. Adams asks about the cause of the argument, Doctor Adams says that Dick had owed him money
for taking care of his squaw who had pneumonia and had
wanted a fight in order not to work off his debt. The real-
life parallel to the events of the story, according to Joseph
Bacon, was this: "I went over to the camp one night and
Dick Boulton was lying on the floor with his head under
the bed. I sent someone over after Doctor Hemingway
and the Doctor came immediately and took care of Dick.
Dick had been drinking something with a kick in it,
probably some kind of dope. Doctor Hemingway told me
that night it was a good thing I called him or else Dick
would have died. The next day I told Dick that the
Doctor had saved his life, but Dick didn't say anything

and went down to Charlevoix that night and died anyway. Maybe he drank some more of the stuff."

In Hemingway's story, the doctor's wife never comes out of her darkened bedroom. Mrs. Hemingway had been blinded by scarlet fever as a child, and although her eyesight returned, she was thereafter sensitive to light and often rested her eyes in a darkened room.

At the end of the story Doctor Adams finds his son in the hemlock woods sitting with his back against a tree, reading a book. Both the young Nick Adams and the young Ernest Hemingway loved to read. An old nurse of Hemingway's was warned by Doctor Hemingway not to let Ernest have any books at night. She remembered:

> *Each evening I'd search his cabin and take away all the books. When I'd tuck him in, he'd say good night, as sweet as could be, then in the morning I'd find books stuffed under the mattress, in the pillowcase, everywhere. He read all the time—and books way beyond his years.*[6]

In the story the doctor takes his son's book and pockets it. That Nick would rather be with his father than go back to the cottage where his mother wants him is understandable. Doctor Adams and his son then go hunting for black squirrels, just as Ernest Hemingway and his father often did. But as the son accompanies his father through the woods, he is downhearted with the knowledge that his father had not stood up to Dick Boulton.

The relationship between Ernest Hemingway's parents was unusual and obviously left some lifelong marks on their son. Doctor Hemingway was a man of practicality and intellect who loved the outdoors and its creatures. Mrs. Hemingway had an artistic temperament, shirked her housewifely responsibilities, and abhorred nature in the raw.

Doctor Hemingway never liked to see his children sitting or reading, preferring them to be active. Probably his father's zest for physical activity, coupled with his mother's inflexibility where her own wishes were concerned, drove Ernest as a child to his own living quarters near the family's summer cottage, then, when he was in his early teens, to a tent of his own in the woods, and finally, when he was a young man, to living with other families in Horton Bay. Doctor Hemingway insisted that his children be with him when he chopped wood, canned fruit, molded bullets, or made candles. All these things might have been interesting to a child doing them himself, but were probably boring to a captive audience.

Mrs. Hemingway not only was different from her husband, but from the norm for upper-middle-class women of her day. She was, in essence, a frustrated career woman. As a child, she often accompanied her mother to the opera, learned to play the organ and piano, and sang in the choir at St. Paul's Episcopal Cathedral in Chicago. All of this was no doubt part of a planned program conceived by a mother ambitious to point her daughter toward an operatic career. Marcelline Hemingway Sanford wrote that Grandmother Hall would not let the future Mrs. Hemingway into the kitchen, saying: "Don't soil your hands with cooking. You tend to your practicing. There is no use any woman getting into the kitchen if she can help it."[7] Grace Hall Hemingway heeded her mother's advice; she never went into the kitchen if she could help it. Instead, she forced her husband into the kitchen.

Grace Hall met Doctor Clarence Hemingway in 1894 and, after a short period of courtship, he proposed to her. Miss Hall accepted, but in the fall of 1895 she went to New York to study with Madame Cappianni instead of staying in Oak Park to be near her fiancé. In New York she received considerable acclaim and the promise of a career which, unfulfilled, festered within her for the rest of her life. Grace Ernestine (she used the feminine version of her father's name as her professional middle name) Hall sang in Madison Square Garden and was offered a contract with the Metropolitan Opera. Her later musings about her lost operatic career were not mere imaginings.

Madame Cappianni urged Miss Hall to accept a contract and remain in New York, but the young Doctor Hemingway bombarded her with letters pleading that she return to Oak Park and marry him in the fall. Her father wanted her to go to Europe with him that summer, and she did. While on her European trip, Grace Hall decided to buy a trousseau instead of gowns for concert appearances. She returned to Oak Park late in August and was married on October 1, 1896.

Doctor and Mrs. Hemingway had six children—Marcelline, Ernest, Ursula, Madelaine (Sunny), Carol, and Leicester. But Mrs. Hemingway, even if she became an indifferent wife and mother, never became a housewife. Mrs. Wesley (Kathryn) Dilworth described Mrs. Hemingway as she knew her when Ernest was growing up: "She studied grand opera, but gave it up to marry Doctor Hemingway. She always talked about giving up her career to have children. She thought she was like Madame Schumann-Heink. She gave music lessons. A girl always took care of the children. Doctor Hemingway did also, and you never saw Mrs. Hemingway with the children, it was always the Doctor. She was large, 5'7" or 5'8", had grey hair, and was attractive."

In an interview, a former nurse of the Hemingways also described Ernest's unhappy home life, which was caused by the reversed and unhealthy roles of his parents.

"Their house was always a mess," she said. "Mrs. Hemingway brought everything up from Chicago in boxes. We used to meet them at the station. There were big trains then. Fourteen-car Pullmans, five and six a

Ernest Hemingway in his Italian uniform decorated with a medal. Taken at Walloon Lake in the summer of 1919 when he was still recovering from his war wounds and using a cane.

Above: Carl Bacon, who was fictionalized in "Ten Indians." Taken on Bacon farm overlooking Hemingway property and Walloon Lake. *Below:* Schoolhouse on Resort Pike Road described in "Ten Indians."

Above left: Joseph Bacon, *center*, in his blacksmith shop as he looked when Ernest Hemingway fictionalized him in "Ten Indians." *Below:* An oil painting of the Bacon farm by Ernest Hemingway's mother. (Her signature, "Hall Hemingway," is in the lower-right-hand corner.) The same scene is described in detail in "Ten Indians" and "Fathers and Sons."

Above: A tintype taken in the 1890's of the Stroud house in Horton Bay with the mill, a lumber schooner, and the bay and point in the background. "In the old days Hortons Bay was a lumbering town. No one who lived in it was out of sound of the big saws in the mill by the lake. . . . The lumber schooners came into the bay and were loaded with the cut of the mill that stood stacked in the yard."—"Up in Michigan." *Lower right:* Stroud house today.

Ed Pailthorp —

For Dutch Pailthorp
to whom J told this
story in the winter of
1919-20 in Petoskey,
Michigan

from his old
friend
Ernie Hemingway.

An inscription in the front of "Dutch" Pailthorp's copy of *A Farewell to Arms*.

Ernest Hemingway in Italy, 1918, before
he was wounded. He gave this photograph to Grace Quinlan.

Top: Horton Bay. Dilworth cottage, "Pinehurst," setting of "Up in Michigan."

Bottom: Scene outside of Petoskey described in "Ten Indians." Resort Pike Road looking across Little Traverse Bay.

day. Petoskey was the end of the line, but you never saw so much junk as when the Hemingways got here. Some of those boxes would sit around all summer still packed, but we always found those gingersnaps. She'd make those up at home and haul them all the way up here. She was a singer. Big woman, sounded like Schumann-Heink. She had a little studio across the lake so she could get away from the noise. We always figured it was the other way around. Dr. Hemingway did most of the cooking. He'd fix the kids' breakfast and then give the Mrs. her breakfast in bed. We saw a lot of Ernie when he was a kid, but later on, not so much. He went off in the woods and he read a lot. He was sort of a loner. Always took that pup tent of his and went fishing somewhere alone."[8]

Ursula Hemingway Jepson, who now lives in Hawaii, wrote in a recent letter: "My grandmother had four sons and she taught them all to cook. Our dad enjoyed it and we did too, especially on rainy days we'd beg him to make doughnuts—one of his specialties. He was years ahead of all the men who now insist on taking over the kitchen or the barbecue pit in the suburbs.

"All the boxes (and there were many) that came to Walloon each year stemmed from the annual orders to Montgomery Ward for all sorts of canned and other foodstuffs to supplement the 'grocery boats' twice weekly visit to our cottage."

Once, Mrs. Hemingway told her oldest daughter, Marcelline: "You know, dear, Schumann-Heink is now taking the place I might have had in opera."[9] The irony of the story of this woman who felt she had missed fame and greatness was that she had achieved fame indirectly, but apparently never realized it. Few people today recognize the name Schumann-Heink, but practically any literate person in the world would have been able to recognize the woman introduced as "the mother of Ernest Hemingway."

Hadley, Ernest Hemingway's first wife (now Mrs. Paul Scott Mower), knew Doctor and Mrs. Hemingway and summed up the relationship between Ernest and his mother when she said: "She had very strong feelings, but she didn't understand the feelings of her son."

Hemingway's other parental story, "Fathers and Sons," published eight years after "The Doctor and the Doctor's Wife," is about a mature Nicholas Adams and his son, who is about the age that Nick was in "Indian Camp." Nick describes himself as thirty-eight in this story, but the flashbacks to his childhood in Michigan cover the period from the time he was about ten through seventeen. "Fathers and Sons" derived its title, but not its context, from the Turgenev novel of the same name.

"Fathers and Sons" opens with Nick and his son driving through a countryside which seems, from the description of red dirt, second-growth timber, and cotton plants, to be in the southern part of the United States. As he drives along, Nick thinks first of hunting, which his father taught him, and then starts thinking about his father.

Nick remembers first, not his father's large frame, his nose hooked like a hawk's, his broad shoulders, or the beard hiding a weak chin, but his deep-set eyes. Nick knew that his father had keener eyesight than most other people, and he considered it one of his father's great gifts. (Doctor Hemingway was shorter than Ernest and had finer features, but they definitely looked like father and son in all their photographs.)

Nick then remembers standing on one shore of the lake (which could be on the opposite side of Walloon Lake from the Hemingway cottage) where his father could see Nick's sister Dorothy, who had raised the flag and walked out onto the dock. Nick remembers having looked across the lake and seen the wooded shoreline with the higher timber behind and the point that guarded the bay, but he could not see the flagpole or dock. He could see only the beach and the curve of the shore.

Then Nick remembers his father as being both nervous and sentimental and that, being sentimental, he was abused. Doctor Hemingway, from reports, had these traits. Nick felt that his father had much bad luck and had died in a trap he had helped only a little to set. Nick felt "they had all betrayed him in their various ways before he died. All sentimental people are betrayed so many times. Nick could not write about him yet, although he would, later . . ."[10]

Hemingway did fictionalize his father later in *For Whom the Bell Tolls*. In that book, the hero, Robert Jordon, says that his father committed suicide, as Doctor Hemingway did in 1928. Pilar, as a guerilla and a peasant who can understand this phenomenon only within the limits of her own experience, wonders if he was being tortured. Jordan answers with a metaphor that it was to avoid torture and changes the subject. His father shot himself with a pistol, Robert reminisces later. He feels that he understands it, but does not approve of it. This was probably Ernest Hemingway's attitude when he remembered his own father's death.

Joseph Bacon said: "Doc shot himself with a revolver in his bedroom at his house in Oak Park. He had an ailment similar to diabetes. He always hated to see his patients suffer and he said he'd never do the same Once when we were riding around the lake in their boat, the doctor said, 'A sane person doesn't commit suicide.'" Bacon thought that Doctor Hemingway killed himself because he was worried about his wife, his children, and his finances.

After remembering his father's puritanical attitudes

about sex, Nick's thoughts digress to the remembrance that his father had the finest pair of eyes he had ever seen and that he had loved his father very much for a long time. Nick felt that knowing how it had all ended, even the conjuring up of the earliest times before things went wrong, gave him no nostalgic pleasure. The next lines are painfully autobiographical, and Hemingway used "he" instead of "Nick" throughout this section. The fictional "he" (Nick) thinks that "he" will get rid of his bad memories about his father's death by writing about them, because "he" had gotten rid of many things by writing about them.

Continuing to use the "he," Hemingway wrote that it was still too early for "him" to write about his father, because too many people were still alive. The fictional "he" tries to think of something else, because he cannot do anything about his father now, even though he has thought it through many times. Then Hemingway wrote about the undertaker's job on Nick's father's face. The undertaker had just repaired the face, but Nick knows that the face of the dead man had made itself and had settled rapidly in the "last three years." Again Hemingway wrote: "It was a good story but there were still too many people alive for him to write it."[11]

The story of Doctor Hemingway's death was a "good story," but an unhappy one which Hemingway never wrote. What happened to the sentimental man? What was the trap that "he had helped only a little to set," which had killed him? How was he "betrayed?" What events in the "last three years" had led up to the morning of December 6, 1928, when Dr. Clarence Edmonds Hemingway walked into his bedroom in Oak Park and shot himself in the head with a Civil War revolver?

Joseph Bacon described in colloquial language what happened to Mrs. Hemingway in the three years which preceded the doctor's death. Bacon's statement discloses a never-before-mentioned situation which might have contributed to Doctor Hemingway's depression. "Mrs. Hemingway lost her mind when she went through the change of life. When she was painting out in my orchard, she was a little off her rocker. Doctor Hemingway was down in Chicago then, and he told me to wire him if anything went wrong. Once, Mrs. Hemingway got out of hand, and I wired the Doctor. He came up immediately, and afterwards told me, 'You know most people would put her in a sanatorium or lock her up, but I just won't do it.' This was a few years before he committed suicide."

In 1925 Doctor and Mrs. Hemingway went to Florida. They invested their entire savings in booming Florida real estate and then took out a mortgage on their house in Oak Park. The Doctor soon had difficulty meeting the continual payments on the lots plus the interest on the mortgage. On top of these troubles, he became diabetic, which affected him deeply, because he had always been a healthy man. He was also burdened with the knowledge that the relentless demands on his income left no cushion for his children's education.

In the spring of 1928 the Hemingways traveled to Florida to make the disappointing discovery that their land had not increased in value. On the Florida trip the Hemingways accidentally ran into their son Ernest in Key West and were reconciled after their estrangement over Ernest's divorce from Hadley and marriage to Pauline Pfeiffer. On returning to Oak Park, Doctor Hemingway's physical condition deteriorated, but he continued to work relentlessly.

Several people in Michigan said that one of the contributing factors to Doctor Hemingway's depression was his need for money and the fact that he owed money to his brother George. According to Marcelline, Doctor Hemingway had asked George for a loan, but his brother had turned him down for business reasons. George Hemingway felt that his brother had overexpanded and should sell some of his Florida property instead of incurring another debt.

On the morning of December sixth, Doctor Hemingway had a pain in his foot which he suspected was caused by gangrene, a result of his diabetes. When he came home for lunch that day, he went upstairs and shot himself with his father's pistol.

Leicester Hemingway wrote that his father had owed a sum of money to a relative (possibly George Hemingway) and had signed a note which was coming due. The "relative" was unsympathetic and requested the note be paid. (This coincides with the statements of the people in Michigan who knew both Doctor and George Hemingway.) According to Leicester, the doctor had written to Ernest for the money. Ernest sent the money immediately. The letter containing the money came on December sixth, and Doctor Hemingway carried it upstairs with him in his final hour, but never opened it.

In "Fathers and Sons" an interlude about the Indians interrupts Nicholas Adams's thoughts about his father. As Nick Adams drives with his own son in the car, he again begins to think about his father, whom he remembers especially each fall and whenever he sees the lake. Nick feels his father is with him when he is in thickets, on small hills, or when he goes through dead grass. Every fall before he was fifteen, Hemingway and his father would go to Michigan to hunt, and they would always stay with the Bacons at their farm. But Nick remembers that after he was fifteen he shared nothing with his father. This was probably also true of Ernest and his father.

Nick then remembers how his father sweated in the summer doing manual work which he loved and Nick hated. Joseph Bacon also remembered a time when Doctor and Ernest Hemingway worked at manual labor. "One day when my son, Earl, and I were hauling shale, Doctor and Ernie Hemingway came up to help and spread the gravel. It was a hot day, and we were all working out in the sun on the road. I looked at the Doctor, and he was pale and looked sick. I told him to go over and sit in the shade. Then I looked at Ernie, and he was about ready to pass out, too. I said, 'Enough of this today,' and they stopped working. They just weren't used to real hard work."

"Fathers and Sons" ends with a conversation between the father (Nick) and the son about the grandfather. Nick remembers that Doctor Adams was a good shot, and that his father's father had been a great wing shot. Doctor Hemingway was supposed to have been an excellent wing shot, as was his father, Ernest's grandfather. About Ernest Hemingway's son Gregory, Malcolm Cowley wrote: "He is good in his studies, but his father complains that his growing interest in books is likely to be the ruin of a superb wing shot."[12]

"Fathers and Sons" is one of Hemingway's most autobiographical short stories. Everything that he wrote about Nick's father was true also of Doctor Hemingway, and the description of the northern Michigan countryside is completely accurate. This poignant story has a structure of tight, almost musical, composition. It opens with the father, Nick, and his son, then has a flashback to the father's father, followed by a flashback to Nick's first love, and then returns to Nick and his son in the present. Hemingway placed the father's death and Nick's awakening of love in flashbacks following one another and framed them by the experience of his own father-son relationship. This interplay continues when Nick again goes in his memory from the present to thoughts of his father. His son brings him back to the present by a question, but the question is about the Ojibwas, which again immediately throws Nick's thoughts into the past, and he again remembers his first love. The young son, with another question, makes Nick think of his father and even of his grandfather. At the end of the story the past joins the present, just as the great-grandfather, grandfather, father, and son form one line which connects them all.

Riding the Rails

Two of Hemingway's Michigan stories are about experiences encountered while hitching rides on freight trains, the only way to travel, except by water or horse and wagon, available to the young writer in that then wild country. In one story, "The Battler," Nick is hitching freights by himself; in the other, "The Light of the World," he has a companion. The setting of "The Battler" is on and beside the tracks of the Grand Rapids & Indiana Railroad, in a tamarack swamp between the towns of Kalkaska and Mancelona. "The Light of the World" is set in a railroad station on the same railroad tracks, probably in the town of Kalkaska.

"The Battler" was published first in *In Our Time*. Nick Adams was either seventeen or nineteen. Nick has left home at the beginning of the story. He was knocked from a freight train by a brakeman, and as he walks along the tracks to the next town, he is attracted to a campfire flickering in the darkness. Nick finds Ad Francis, a punch-drunk, ex-prizefighter and his Negro companion, Bugs. Nick is invited to join them for dinner, but then Ad becomes hostile and wants to fight with Nick. Bugs knocks Ad out with a blackjack, and Nick again starts walking up the tracks.

Malcolm Cowley in his article "A Portrait of Mister Papa" wrote that Hemingway "wasn't happy at high school and twice he ran away from home."[1] Maybe on one of those trips Hemingway had the experience which inspired "The Battler."

Hemingway's sister Marcelline wrote about her brother hiking to Michigan, not running away from home, when he was in high school.

> *Twice before this at the beginning of vacations, Ernest had walked up to Walloon Lake after taking the boat across from Chicago to the lower part of Michigan. Once Louis Clarahan went with him, and the other time, as I recall, Harold Sampson made the long hike— over three hundred miles—with him. The boys camped along the way, sleeping in pup tents, cooking their own meals, swimming or fishing as they pleased . . .*[2]

Ursula Hemingway Jepson added an interesting family footnote when she wrote in a private letter: "As to the 'running away' business—even Marcelline did it once, and I did it several times and met Ernie in Petoskey."

Stanley Van Hoesen, who lived in Horton Bay in 1919, also remembered the time when "Ernie walked from Chicago to Horton Bay," and added, "at this time Hemingway had a steel plate in his leg and was limping." Therefore, it must have been a post–World War I experience.

John McConnell remembered driving down the main road which leads to the Hemingway cottage and seeing a limping man walking along the road. It was a cold, blustery night in March. "We asked him if he wanted a ride, and he said 'no.' I then recognized Ernie and asked him what he was doing up here at this time of year. He said he was going down to their cottage and stay there. I told him that it was all boarded up, but he said he guessed as how he would have to break in then."

Joseph Bacon also remembered that "Ernie came up to the cottage one March right after the War." This is possible, since Hemingway returned from Europe on January

21, 1919. "Ernie stayed at the cottage one night but just about froze to death, so when he came up to the farmhouse the next day, we put him up."

In "The Battler" the first thing Nick Adams does, after he is thrown from the train, is feel his knee. This might be just because he landed on it. If this is an autobiographical story modeled from Hemingway's own experiences, he would be concerned about his war-wounded limb and be prompted to bathe it, as Nick does.

Nick had boarded the freight train near Walton Junction. It had gone "through Kalkaska as it started to get dark" and had come "nearly to Mancelona," which indicates Nick was traveling northward from Chicago to Walloon Lake. The action in "The Battler" could have been taken from either a pre– or post–World War I experience of Hemingway's. The year is not important to the story.

"The Battler" is essentially the story of the young man's encounter with a world unknown to his parents. Nick answers in the negative Ad Francis's specific question of whether he is "tough." But when Francis observes that "all you kids are tough," Nick notes, "You [sic] got to be tough."[3] The young Hemingway, by hitching rides on freights, dealing with tough strangers, and testing his strength of power and will, became "tough" in order to exist in the strange world outside of his family's community.

The other Michigan story which is set along the Grand Rapids & Indiana Railroad tracks is "The Light of the World." The story first appeared in *Winner Take Nothing* on October 27, 1933. Hemingway, in his preface to *The Short Stories of Ernest Hemingway*, listed this story among the seven stories which he liked best, although he said that "nobody else ever liked it."

Nick and a friend of his, Tom, find themselves in the midst of ten men and five women. The women are prostitutes, three fat ones and two thin ones with peroxided hair.

Of the ten men, there are four silent Indians and six white men, one a homosexual cook. In the course of the story, Nick becomes involved in a discussion of adultery, fornication, homosexual and heterosexual "perversions," converses somewhat professionally with the large prostitute, to whom he is attracted, and successfully escapes the advances of the cook, whom one of the men calls a "sister."

Hemingway probably received the inspiration for the character of the cook in "The Light of The World" from a cook who worked at the lumber camp across the lake from the Hemingway cottage. The real cook, whom Marcelline Hemingway Sanford described, seems similar to the one in "The Light of the World," who "Puts lemon juice on his hands" and "wouldn't get them into dishwater for anything."[4] Mrs. Sanford wrote:

> Once in a while we were invited into the mill cook-house, where the camp cook, a mild-mannered old fellow, an apron tied over his pants, apologetically wiped his damp fingers on his apron and said in a gentle, almost ladylike voice:
>
> "Pardon me if my hands are wet. I've just been making biscuits and you know how it is to keep your hands clean in the kitchen."
>
> Often he gave Ernie and me a doughnut or a sugar cookie. They were delicious.
>
> The old man was a good cook and the men liked his grub. But the contrast between this neat, gentle, kindly soul and the rough, unshaven, tobacco-spitting lumberjacks was so great that it is no wonder they made fun of him behind his back. The millhands called him "the old lady" and "the maid of the moist palm."[5]

Possibly the lumbermen called the cook a "sister" also. The cook who seemed a "gentle, kindly soul" to his sister, probably appeared in a different light to Ernest Hemingway, who had had more contact with the world outside of his parents' middle-class environment.

At the beginning of the story, Nick and Tom (or "Tommy," as he is sometimes called in the story) enter a bar. In the following section Tom almost gets into a fight with the bartender, but Nick placates the bartender and makes Tom leave the bar. John McConnell knew an Indian named Tom who lived at the lumber camp, was a friend of Hemingway's, and was about his age.

Joseph Bacon knew a Dan Mitchell, who married a Tabeshaw girl, and a Tommy Mitchell, who lived in the Indian Camp. Tommy's father was also a member of the Tabeshaw family, but Tommy always gave his name as Mitchell. Tommy Mitchell's father later lived in Petoskey, when Tommy was a teen-ager, and was one of the drunken Indians who passed out on the railroad tracks and was run over by a train.

Hemingway did not give the name of the town where "The Light of the World" is located, but he did give an impression of it. He wrote of its smell of hides and tan bark and big sawdust piles. This could be the town of Kalkaska, which has a bar opposite the train station and used to be a lumber town. The fictional homosexual cook is waiting to take the train to Cadillac, which is south of Kalkaska. In the story the heavy prostitute is from Mancelona and is probably returning there. Mancelona is the next train stop north of Kalkaska.

The central discussion of the story is between two whores about a fighter named Steve or Stanley Ketchel (they disagree about his first name) from Cadillac. The thin one lies about her relationship with the fighter, but it becomes clear that Alice, the three-hundred-and-fifty-pound woman, is the one who really knew Ketchel. Stanley Ketchel was a real-life heavyweight fighter who lost the championship title fight to Jack Johnson in 1909 in Colma, California. Again Hemingway wove real names and incidents into a story, this time they were well-known names of famous fighters and a famous championship fight.

At one point in the story Nick says that he and Tommy are "seventeen and nineteen." Hemingway at both seventeen and nineteen was a close friend of the Tommy from the lumber camp, would often "hitch freights," had started to drink at bars, and was in Michigan at the end of summer, when "the puddles of water in the road were freezing at the edges." It is very possible that Hemingway encountered sordid characters like the ones in the story when he rode the rails in order to fish, hunt, or just travel.

The title of this story is taken from Matthew 5:14: "Ye are the light of the world. A city that is set on a hill cannot be hid." Hemingway's meaning could be ironic, suggesting that all of the sordid people in the train station are "the light of the world," or he could mean that the truth spoken by Alice "cannot be hid."

In one of his letters, written on July 31, 1933, to Maxwell Perkins, Hemingway suggested that this story has some points in common with Maupassant's "La Maison Tellier."[6] Two years later Hemingway listed sixteen titles which he would rather read again than be assured of a million-dollar annual income; one of those titles was Maupassant's "The House of Madame Tellier."[7]

Although Guy de Maupassant's style foreshadowed Hemingway's (not necessarily the style, though, of "The Light of the World"), the stories seem to have few points in common, contrary to Hemingway's own suggestion. "La Maison Tellier" is about a peasant woman who is the "Madame" of a house of prostitution in a small town in Normandy. She takes her entire establishment of five girls to a family Confirmation in a nearby town, meanwhile closing her house of business. At the Confirmation the girls become emotional, causing the entire congregation to weep. The priest and other inhabitants of the town have no idea about the profession of Madame Tellier and the girls and are impressed by their religious fervor. When the girls and the Madame return to their house of business, the leading men of the town join them in a champagne celebration.

"The Light of the World" has prostitutes in it, but they are more realistic creatures than Maupassant's gay girls. The men in Hemingway's story are rough lumberjacks and Indians, not the "respectable" burghers of Normandy. Except for the small point that the girls in Madame Tellier's establishment traveled by "second-class carriage" and Hemingway's prostitutes are waiting in a railway station, and that both stories show that a woman's sense of truth and reality is not a true reality, the stories have little in common. But from a general point of view, both Maupassant and Hemingway seem to see the underside of life in a humorous way, and both present their worlds in a straight, down-to-earth style: maybe these are the points which Hemingway felt these two stories have in common.

The Bacons and Prudence

Two of Hemingway's Michigan stories are based on his relationships with some of his Walloon Lake neighbors: the Bacons, a farming family, and Prudence, the Indian girl of the Indian camp. In the story "Fathers and Sons," a mature Nicholas Adams remembers his first sexual relationship, which had been with the Indian girl. In "Ten Indians" young Nick Adams is riding in the Garners' farm wagon, and he later learns that Prudence has been unfaithful to him.

The story "Ten Indians" was first published in *Men without Women*, a collection of short stories published by Scribner's on October 14, 1927. Hemingway in an interview once said:

> *I wrote "Ten Indians" after writing "The Killers" in Madrid on May 16 when it snowed out the San Isidro bullfights. . . . I had so much juice I thought maybe I was going crazy and I had about six other stories to write. So I got dressed and walked to Fornos, the old bull fighter's cafe, and drank coffee and then came back and wrote "Ten Indians." This made me very sad and I drank some brandy and went to sleep.*[1]

Why did this story make him very sad? Probably for two reasons: one was the remembrance of his unhappy home situation, and the other was that it make him remember how he felt after his first girl friend had been unfaithful to him.

The "Joe Garner" in "Ten Indians" resembles Joe Bacon in real life, and everything in this story points to the fact that Joe Garner is modeled after Joe Bacon. Joseph Bacon's father built a log cabin and began his farm on Walloon Lake in 1878. Joe Bacon said that he sold some lakefront property to Doctor Hemingway in 1895, which differs from both Marcelline's date of 1898 and Leicester's of 1900.

Mrs. George Depew, the former Myrtle Dale, lived in 1960 on Depew Road, which is about a mile behind the Hemingway cottage. A lifelong resident of the area, she knew both the Bacon family and Prudence. Mrs. Depew remembered: "the Bacon barn burnt down about twenty-five years ago, and the house was torn down afterwards. The Bacons settled there in 1880. The first resort cottage on Walloon Lake was built in 1878. The Bacon farmhouse was frame and painted white while the barn was painted red. The Bacon property ran down to the lake right next to the Hemingway land."

John McConnell also remembered the Bacon family: " 'Doc' Hemingway drove the last spike at Bacon's barn-raising and was proud of that and talked about it a lot. Everyone said, 'the Bacons feed the Hemingways, but they get their doctoring for free!' Doctor Hemingway kept a garden over at their place on the other side of the lake that they called 'Longfield,' because of its long field. One summer Ernie rowed around to the cottages on the lake and came up to the hotel with a load of vegetables he was trying to sell. So the Bacons didn't supply the Hemingways with all their food. Joe Bacon always judges the chickens at the Emmet County Fair and says, 'I've never missed a fair.' He must be about ninety now."

In "Ten Indians" Nick is driving home from Petoskey in the Garners' big wagon. As they drive along, they pass nine drunken Indians on the road. (The tenth Indian of the title is Nick's girl, Prudence.) Joe Garner pulls the horses to a halt and drags one Indian out of the wheel rut, where he had fallen asleep with his face in the sand.

Joe Bacon remembered one night when he and his family were returning home in what he also called the "big wagon," and they passed a squaw who was "dead drunk and lying face down in the middle of the road." Mrs. Bacon said, according to her husband, "Just run her over, she ain't worth nothing no how." Joe Bacon stopped the wagon and lifted the Indian woman to the side of the road. The next morning, when he asked the squaw about it, she did not remember anything of the night before.

Billy Tabeshaw, who appeared before in "The Doctor and the Doctor's Wife" and "Sepi Jingan," is again mentioned in this story. Carl Garner wonders whether one of the drunken Indians was Billy Tabeshaw, but either Nick Adams or Frank Garner (the speaker is not identified) says that it is not Billy. But Carl thinks that the Indian's pants looked like Billy's, and the unidentified speaker (probably Nick) then makes the pronouncement that Indians all wear the same type of pants.

The route of the farm wagon going from Petoskey to Resort Pike Road in "Ten Indians" can be followed today by the same landmarks described in the story. As they drive along in the wagon, the road turns off the main highway and leads up into the hills. At this point the horses have to pull hard, and the boys have to get out and walk on the sandy road. Then Nick looks back from the hilltop by the schoolhouse and sees the lights of Petoskey and, off across Little Traverse Bay, the lights of Harbor Springs. (Hemingway sometimes spelled "Harbour Springs" with the British "u," but all records and maps indicate that it has always been spelled "Harbor Springs.") In the story the boys climb back into the wagon, and Joe Garner suggests that gravel should be put

THE BACONS AND PRUDENCE [99]

on that part of the road, probably to insure better traction.

Joseph Bacon was able to pinpoint the entire trip, since three roads offer a route past a schoolhouse and a night view of both Harbor Springs and Petoskey. "When we came from Petoskey in the horse and wagon," Bacon said, "we would come up Washout Road then cross over to Resort Pike where the Greig schoolhouse is on the corner." The original landmarks on this most direct and logical of the three possible routes are exactly as they were described by Hemingway in "Ten Indians." The young Hemingway had traveled with Joseph Bacon in his wagon over the exact route which Joe Garner and Nick Adams follow in the story.

Earlier in the story Hemingway mentioned the two Garner boys, "Carl" and "Frank." Joseph Bacon had six children, one boy named Earl and another named Carl, but he did not have a son named Frank. Carl Garner, who teases the young Nick Adams about his Indian girl, is the principal speaker of the two Garner boys. In real life, Carl Bacon was Hemingway's friend. The experience which formed the inspiration for this story probably happened when Hemingway was about sixteen or seventeen. Joseph Bacon recalled that "Ernie and Carl were always playing together and making a mess out in the wheat shucks when they were young."

But when the action in this story took place, Nick Adams and Carl Garner were not interested in playing in the wheat shucks. They had a more interesting topic of conversation, girls. In this story the girl discussed is the Indian girl "Prudence Mitchell."

Mrs. George Depew taught school in the one-room schoolhouse of Resort District in 1911, when Hemingway was twelve. At this little schoolhouse, which has since been torn down, Mrs. Depew had in her classes a little Indian girl, Prudence Boulton, who was about ten years old, which meant she was two years younger than Hemingway. Prudence Boulton, according to the people who knew her, was Dick Boulton's daughter which would make her one-fourth French and three-fourths Indian. As a child of ten, Prudence was supposed to have had nice skin, long, black hair, and to be pretty.

Another Indian family at the camp was the Mitchells, but they did not have a Prudence Mitchell among them. The Mitchells were related to the Boultons, since Dan Mitchell's wife was a Tabeshaw and so was Dick Boulton's wife. When Hemingway named Nick's Indian girlfriend, he probably changed Prudence Boulton's last name to Mitchell. Since there were no other girls named "Prudence" living in the Indian camp, Prudence Boulton must have been Hemingway's original model for "Prudence Mitchell." Years later Hemingway gave his wife, Mary, a compliment, by telling her that she had legs "just like Trudy Boulton's."

While Nick, Carl, and Mr. and Mrs. Garner converse, Hemingway describes their progress in the wagon along Resort Pike. At one point when the horses pull hard in the sand, Joe Garner whips them. This is on a steep incline where the horses would have had to pull heavily. Later on in the story the horses trot down a long hill with the wagon jolting. Resort Pike follows the same route today.

In the story Mr. and Mrs. Garner are a happily married couple who tease each other. Their warm relationship is also shown in their attitude toward their children and the neighbor boy, Nick. Their home is a happy home, in contrast to the one of Nick Adams as described in "The Doctor and the Doctor's Wife." When Nick leaves the Garners' farmhouse to go to his own house, Mrs. Garner asks him to send Carl, who is outside unloading the wagon, to the house. When Nick goes down to the barn to thank Joe Garner for the good time he had, Nick casually tells him to tell Carl his mother wants him. It is assumed that Carl will be given this message and go to his mother. The naturalness of this request of the mother and response of the son is in direct contrast to the reactions of Nick to the same request at the end of "The Doctor and the Doctor's Wife."

In "Ten Indians" Nick takes the familiar walk from the Garners' farmhouse to his parents' summer cottage: through the meadow which is below the Garners' barn, over a fence at the end of the meadow, then down through a ravine where he gets his feet wet in the swamp mud. Then he climbs up through the beech woods (which still surround the Hemingway cottage), until he sees the lights of the cottage. (This route is the same one Nick Adams traveled in the story, "Fathers and Sons.") Nick's father is by himself, reading in the kitchen, when Nick comes in and brings Nick his dinner of cold chicken, milk, and huckleberry pie. His mother does not appear in this story.

As Nick and his father sit in the kitchen talking, Nick asks his father what he had done during the day. The father answers that he went for a walk near the Indian camp; when Nick quizzes him as to whether he had seen anyone, Doctor Adams notes noncommittally that all of the Indians were in town getting drunk. When Nick presses him, he answers that he had seen Nick's friend Prudie "threshing around" in the woods with a boy named Frank Washburn.

Nick begins crying when his father leaves the room. When Doctor Adams sees his son in tears, he tries to comfort him by offering him some more pie and then suggesting that Nick go to bed. In his room Nick feels that his heart is broken, but he feels well enough to observe that a cool wind has come up. After a while he forgets to think about Prudence and falls asleep. In the middle of the night Nick awakes to hear the wind in the trees, but goes back to sleep. By morning a strong wind is blowing, and the waves are coming far up the beach, and he is awake for a long time before he remembers his grief.

A poem, "Along With Youth," which Hemingway wrote in Paris and which appeared in *Three Stories and Ten Poems*, captures the same sentiments about lost youth and young love that are aroused in "Ten Indians." Most of the images in the poem come from northern Michigan, and some are the same as in the story.

In "Fathers and Sons" Hemingway described a route that he had often taken from the family cottage on Walloon Lake to the hemlock woods behind the Indian camp. Nick Adams follows the same route to the trysting place with the Indian girl. The route can be followed on foot today, although the fences and the Bacons' barn have disappeared. The pine-needle loam is still underfoot in the hemlock woods behind the Hemingway cottage and fallen logs still crumble into wood dust. Pieces of splintered wood still hang like javelins from a large, lightning-struck tree, probably not the same one the young boy passed, but one which brings to mind the tree in the story. The small creek runs nearby, crossed by a log. If you were to slip from the log, you would still step into the black swamp muck.

Proceeding northwest to the left, you would still find the swampy creek bottom. The fence that the young Hemingway climbed over has disappeared, but you still come out of the woods and on to the place where the field for grazing used to be. The field is now overgrown and full of wild flowers. You go by the barn, over another fence, past the house, and down the sandy road which went into the woods. The sandy road, which is still hot underfoot in summer, runs from the site of the former farmhouse to the woods, but now it runs past rows of planted Christmas trees.

The Bacon farmhouse no longer stands on the site, but Joseph Bacon had an oil painting of it. In his small house in Petoskey in 1960, he dug through a pile of assorted souvenirs of his past, which were stacked in a corner of his

living room, and came out with a painting of his home-
stead. When asked, not volunteering the information himself, who had done the painting, Bacon answered, "Mrs.
Hemingway." Without knowing it, Ernest Hemingway's
mother had painted in oils the exact landscape which her
son had meticulously described in both "Ten Indians" and
"Fathers and Sons."

But Nick's trip in "Fathers and Sons" is not over. After
he passes the Garners' farm, he continues towards his teen-
age Indian girl friend. He goes into the woods on the clay
and shale road, off the main road, which turns to the left,
and goes around the woods and then climbs the hill. The
actual road to the Indian camp was broad at the point
where the Indians slid out the hemlock bark they cut.

Hemingway, with his facility for total recall and accurate description, has caught in "Fathers and Sons," in
eighty-four words, the color, smell, physical appearance,
and purpose of the Indian lumber camp. Other neighbors
and members of the Hemingway family have all described
the Indian camp, but only Ernest was able to capture it as
it was, even predicting its demise, within his eighty-four
words. The hemlock forest around the camp has long since
been destroyed by the Indian barkpeelers, who took the
bark to the tannery in Boyne City, as the Indians did in
Hemingway's story. The buildings of the camp and all of
the Indians have also disappeared. And now nothing remains in the maple woods except grown-over roads and
man-moved earth—roads leading nowhere and useless
earth barricades.

The next section of the story is a description of what
Theodore Bardacke writes is "the one satisfying sexual
relationship of the volume (*Winner Take Nothing*). This
is an adolescent union with a little Indian girl who is
submissive and devoid of any real individual personality."[2]
The Indian girl in this story is called "Trudy," which is
very close to the "Prudence" and "Prudie" of "Ten In-

dians." She has a brother named Billy Gilby, who shoots with Nick's gun while Nick makes love to his sister. The two Indians mention an older half-breed brother named Eddie Gilby, who is seventeen. Trudy's age is established as having been about fifteen at the time of the incident Nick remembers in "Fathers and Sons." This would correspond to the age of Prudence Boulton at the time she and Hemingway were seen together. There was a Billy Mitchell, an Indian who lived at the lumber camp, and the name of the previously mentioned Indian family of Gilberts is similar to Gilby. Prudence Boulton also had a brother Eddy, who was a half-breed, as she was.

Nick makes love to Trudy on a hemlock-needled bed in the woods while Billy, her brother, lies near them. Afterwards, Nick is happy, until Trudy tells him that her older half-brother wants to sleep with his (Nick's) sister. It is all right if Nick has an affair with Trudy, but this is another thing. Equality is over. Nick is furious. He threatens to kill Eddie Gilby, whom he calls a "half-breed bastard." Trudy becomes upset and pleads with Nick not to kill her half-brother, but Nick is enjoying his role and enacts the whole, imaginary murder, even to the point of scalping Eddie Gilby. Billy notes that Nick is just a big bluff, and Nick finally agrees with Trudy that he would not murder Eddie unless he came near the Adams house.

Trudy is relieved and wants to make love again. This time Nick sends Billy away with the gun. After they make love, Trudy wonders whether they had made a baby. When Nick answers negatively, she says in slang that it does not make any difference if she becomes pregnant.

Mrs. Depew, who had taught the ten-year-old Prudence Boulton in the one-room schoolhouse of the Resort District, remembered indistinctly what eventually happened to Prudence: "Prudence never married, but died when she was young. I don't know how, since I was away from home at the time. When I asked them about her, my parents told me that she had died. She never finished high school. Prudence was a pretty girl, but many Indian girls are more attractive when they are young. She had nice skin, long, black hair, and looked like a full-blooded Indian."

Some of the people who knew Prudence said that she died in childbirth, and one even said that the rumor had gone around that it was Ernest Hemingway's child Prudence was carrying. She was buried in Bay Shore, according to her neighbors, and a "priest prayed over her grave."

Nick's little boy in "Fathers and Sons" asks his father about how it was when he used to hunt with the Indians. Nick tells him that his father only gave him three shells, so that he would learn to hunt. Nick adds that he used to go out nearly every day hunting black squirrels with Billy Gilby and Trudy. When his son questions him further about the Indians, Nicholas Adams is unable to tell his son about his sexual experience with Trudy.

When Hemingway wrote about Trudy and his memories of her, he wrote in abbreviated "Indian talk." Later in his life Hemingway often lapsed into Indian talk, which caused some critics, notably Lillian Ross in her *New Yorker* interview, to ridicule him for what they seemed to consider an affectation. Since the young writer had spent many of his formative years among the Ojibwas and had spoken their language, his Indian talk was not an affectation, but an integral part of his own speech and writing patterns.

Nick felt that jokes about Indian girls, old squaws, and the sick-sweet smell they get could not take away what he once felt for Trudy. Hemingway wrote in "Fathers and Sons" about what happened to Indian girls. "Nor what they did finally. It wasn't how they ended. They all ended the same. Long time ago good. Now no good."[3]

Although "what they did finally" could be construed as the actions of Prudence in "Ten Indians," it seems doubtful that Hemingway knew what finally became of Prudence Boulton. Becoming promiscuous and a fat squaw is apparently what became of many pretty, young Indian girls in northern Michigan, but from the testimony of the neighbors this was not Prudence's fate.

The wooden crosses over the remaining Indian graves in the lonely, roadside town of Bay Shore are unmarked. Now Bay Shore is just a few houses in the middle of wild, overgrown fields on the highway from Petoskey to Charlevoix, and none of the people there knew about Prudence Boulton. Indian deaths, births, and marriages were rarely recorded in the 1910's, and neither the Charlevoix nor the Emmet County Courthouse has any records about Prudence Boulton. If Ernest Hemingway did know about Prudence's death, he did not incorporate it into either of his two "Prudence" stories.

SECTION II:
AFTER THE WAR

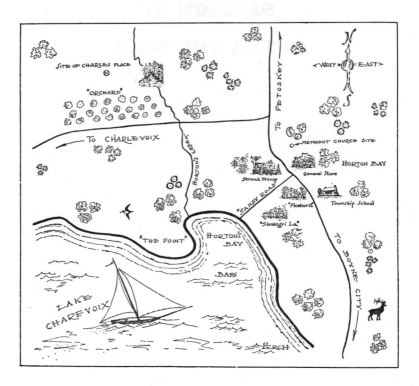

War Wounds

The turning point of Hemingway's early life was the night when he was seriously wounded for the first time near the village of Fossalta, Italy. The date was July 8, 1918, just before his nineteenth birthday.

Up until that midnight, Hemingway's personality, ideas, and point of view were forming, but the shock of being wounded and spending three months recovering in the American Red Cross hospital at Milan fused his character. He now became a writer with something compellingly important to write about—wounds and death. *A Farewell to Arms* was written directly from this experience. Jake Barnes of *The Sun Also Rises* was also wounded in the First World War. The short stories, "Now I Lay Me," "A Way You'll Never Be," and "Soldier's Home," were about a soldier who had been wounded. As late as 1950, in *Across the River and Into the Trees*, the time, place, and the action of the 1918 wound were recreated.

In the short story "Now I Lay Me," which was first published on October 14, 1927, in *Men Without Women*, the nameless main character is lying awake at night, keeping himself awake because he feels that if he were to close his eyes, his soul would go out of his body. Lieutenant Henry in *A Farewell to Arms* had felt himself rush bodily out of himself, float around, and return to his wounded body. Hemingway later told his friend Guy Hickok: "I died then [*recounting his own wound sustained at Fossalta*]. I felt my soul or something coming right out of my body, like you'd pull a silk handkerchief out of a pocket by one corner. It flew around and then came back and went in again and I wasn't dead any more."[1]

In *A Farewell to Arms* Lieutenant Henry is wounded in much the same way that Hemingway was. Hemingway did not remember how he had gotten to the dressing station or that he had carried another wounded soldier to safety, but his actions were described to him the next day by an Italian officer.

The most complete description of how he suffered his war wound is contained in a letter he wrote his parents which was subsequently published in the Chicago *Evening Post* on October 23, 1918.

. . . . .

OAK PARK BOY "SHOT TO PIECES" JOKES ABOUT IT

Ernest Hemingway Suffers 227 Wounds While in Red Cross Service

Thoroly [sic] *typical of the American spirit and the humor that will carry the men over all obstacles is the letter recently received by C. E. Hemingway of Oak Park from his 19-year-old son, Ernest, who is convalesc-ing* [sic] *in an Italian hospital from 227 wounds. The letter was published in Oak Leaves.*

Young Hemingway was working in the editorial de-partment of the Kansas City Star when he volunteered for ambulance driving in the Red Cross. His work was in the mountainous regions of Northern Italy, and late in the summer, when he was working in a front-line trench a shell exploded burying his companion under a trench mortar and inflicting the wounds from which Hemingway is now recovering. The letter follows:

"Dear Folks:—Gee, family, but there must have been a great bubble about my getting shot up. Oak Leaves and the opposition came today and I have begun to think, family, that maybe you didn't appreciate me when I used to reside in the bosom. It's the next best thing to getting killed and reading your own obituary.

Nothing Funny About War

"You know they say there isn't anything funny about this war, and there isn't. I wouldn't say that it was hell, because that's been a bit overworked since General Sherman's time, but there have been about eight times when I would have welcomed hell, just on a chance that it couldn't come up to the phase of war I was experiencing.

"For example, in the trenches, during an attack, when a shell makes a direct hit in a group where you're standing. Shells aren't bad except direct hits: you just take chances on the fragments of the bursts. But when there is a direct hit, your pals get splattered all over you; splattered is literal.

"During the six days I was up in the front line trenches only fifty yards from the Austrians I got the 'rep' of having a charmed life. The 'rep' of having one doesn't mean much, but having one does. I hope I have one. That knocking sound is my knuckles striking the wooden bedtray.

"Well, I can now hold up my hand and say that I've been shelled by high explosives, shrapnel and gas; shot at by trench mortars, snipers and machine guns, and, as an *added attraction, an aeroplane machine gunning the line. I've never had a hand grenade struck rather close. Maybe I'll get a hand grenade later.*

Shot *"Advancing to the Rear"*

"Now, out of all that mess to only get struck by a trench mortar and a machine-gun bullet, while advancing toward the rear, as the Irish say, was fairly lucky. What, Family?

"The 227 wounds I got from the trench mortar didn't hurt a bit at the time, only my feet felt like I had on rubber boots full of water (hot water), and my knee cap was acting queer. The machine-gun bullet just felt like a sharp smack on the leg with an icy snow ball. However, it spilled me. But I got up again and got my wounded into the dugout. I kind of collapsed at the dugout.

"The Italian I had with me had bled all over me, and my coat and pants looked like some one had made currant jelly in them and then punched holes to let the pulp out. Well, my captain, who was a great pal of mine (it was his dugout) said:

"'Poor Hem., he'll be R.I.P. soon!' Rest in peace, that is.

"You see, they thought I was shot thru my chest, because of my bloody coat. But I made them take my coat and shirt off (I wasn't wearing any undershirt), and the old torso was intact. So they said that I would probably live. That cheered me up any amount.

"I told them in Italian that I wanted to see my legs, thos [sic] I was afraid to look at them. So they took off my trousers and the old limbs were still there, but, gee, they were a mess. They couldn't figure out how I had

walked a hundred and fifty yards with such a load, with both knees shot thru and my right shoe punctured in two big places; also over 200 flesh wounds.

Makes Light of Wounds

" 'Oh,' says I, in Italian, 'my captain, it is nothing. In America they all do it. It is thought well not to allow the enemy to perceive that they have captured our goats!' The goat speech required some masterful lingual ability, but I got it across and then went to sleep for a couple of minutes.

"After I came to they carried me on a streatcher three kilometers back to a dressing station. The streatcher bearers had to go over lots, as the road was having the entrails shelled out of it. Whenever a big one would come, wh-e-ee-eeee-whoo-oosh-boom, they would lay me down and get flat.

"My wounds were now hurting like 227 little devils driving nails into the raw. The dressing station had been evacuated during the attack, so I lay for two hours in a stable with its roof shot off, waiting for an ambulance. When it came I ordered it down the road to get the soldiers that had been wounded first. It came back with a load and then they lifted me in.

"The shelling was still pretty thick and our batteries were going off all the time 'way back of us, and the big 350s and 250s going overhead for Austria with a noise like a railway train. Then we'd hear the burst back of the lines. Then, shriek would come a big Austrian shell and then the crack of the burst. But we were giving them more and bigger stuff than they sent.

"Then a battery of field guns would go off just back of the shed—boom-boom! Boom-boom! and the 75s and

*149s would go whimpering over to the Austrian lines.
And the star shells going up all the time and the machine
guns going like riveters—tat-a-tat-tat.*

Left Among "Pals"

"*After a ride of a couple of kilometers in an Italian
ambulance they unloaded me at a dressing station,
where I had a lot of pals among the medical officers.
They gave me a shot of morphine and anti-tetanus
serum and shaved my legs and took twenty-eight shell
fragments varying in size from* [he drew a sketch] *to
about* [another sketch] *in size out of my legs.*

"*Then they did a fine job of bandaging and all shook
hands with me and would have kissed me, but I kidded
them along. Then I stayed five days at a field hospital
and was evacuated to the base hospital here.*

"*I sent you that cable so you wouldn't worry. I have
been in the hospital a month and twelve days and hope
to be out in another month. The Italian surgeons did a
peach of an operation on my right knee joint and my
right foot; took twenty-eight stitches, and assures me
that I will be able to walk as well as ever. The wounds
all healed up clean and there was no infection. He has
my right leg in a plaster splint now, so that will be all
right.*

"*I have some snappy souvenirs that he took out at the
last operation. I wouldn't really be comfortable now
unless I had some pain. The surgeon is going to take the
plaster off in a week now and will allow me on crutches
in ten days. I will have to learn to walk again.*

"*This is the longest letter I have ever written to
anyone and it says the least. Give my love to everybody
that asks about me and as Ma Pettingill says 'Leave us
keep the home fires burning.'*"

. . . . .

From the night he was wounded until the time he was released from the Milan hospital, Hemingway had a dozen operations in all. At the American Red Cross hospital another important event in relation to his writing and development occurred: He fell in love with Agnes von Kurowsky, who was a nurse at the hospital. She was a tall girl, older than her nineteen-year-old lover, and resembled his future wife, Hadley. Ernest had been in love before, contrary to his brother's statement in his book that Agnes was his first love. Hemingway had been loved and left by Prudence Boulton, but he had never considered marrying her. He now wanted to marry Agnes.

But the pattern of his first love prevailed. He returned to the United States on January 21, 1919, and awaited a decision from Agnes on his marriage proposal. The letter came; in it she turned him down.

Hemingway was bitter, and he wrote a short piece, "A Very Short Story," about his love affair with a nurse in Milan. In this cruel story, the nurse has an affair with an Italian major of the battalion stationed in the small town, and she plans to marry him. She breaks the news by letter to the unnamed main character of the story that their love had only been a "boy-girl affair." The "he" in the story contracts gonorrhea from a salesgirl in Chicago and never answers the letter. And the nurse never marries her Italian major. In real life, Agnes von Kurowsky was engaged to an Italian officer after Hemingway left, and she also returned to the United States without marrying the Italian.

Later, when Hemingway wrote *A Farewell to Arms*, he remembered Agnes in a better light, through his character Catherine Barkley, who was based upon her. Not only was the injury scene in *A Farewell to Arms* drawn, with few changes, from his own experiences, but so was most of the rest of the book. After the War, when he lived in Petoskey, Hemingway told his friend, E. G. "Dutch" Pailthorp, the true story of his injury and his love affair with the nurse. According to Pailthorp, the story was similar to that of *A Farewell to Arms*, except for the ending when the couple began rowing for Switzerland. Years later when Hemingway returned to Michigan and saw "Dutch" Pailthorp, they discussed the book. Hemingway admitted that it was the same true story he had told Dutch after the First World War and that he "had made up the ending." At that time (in the early fifties), Hemingway autographed Pailthorp's copy of *A Farewell to Arms* with this inscription: "Here is a *Farewell to Arms*, the story which I told you. Ernest Hemingway."

Just as he had used his own experiences to write his Michigan stories, Hemingway also incorporated his experience with Agnes at the hospital at Milan and their trips in the surrounding countryside into *A Farewell to Arms*. Miss De Long, the director of the Milan hospital, was the basis for Miss Van Campen in the book, and both real and fictional nurses were upset about the cognac bottles in the patient's closet. Miss Elsie MacDonald, Miss De Long's assistant, always took Hemingway's part against the director, as did Miss Gage in the book. The final form of *A Farewell to Arms* did not emerge full-blown in Hemingway's mind until ten years later, in 1928, after he had lived through many of the experiences that the novel's hero and heroine do. Not long before that, his second wife, Pauline, gave birth to their son, Patrick, by Caesarean section. She almost died during the delivery. This ordeal undoubtedly suggested the fictional Catherine Barkley's pregnancy, the death of the fictional son, and Catherine's death after a Caesarean. Hemingway rewrote the final page of *A Farewell to Arms* thirty-nine agonizing times until he felt it was just right.

The character of Jake Barnes in *The Sun Also Rises* lead many people to speculate on the nature of Hemingway's war wound. When Hemingway was asked by George Plimpton, in the *Paris Review* interview, about

Jake Barnes, "who is emasculated precisely as is a steer," Hemingway answered:

> *Who ever said Jake was 'emasculated precisely as is a steer?' Actually he had been wounded in quite a different way and his testicles were intact and not damaged. Thus he was capable of all normal feelings as a man but incapable of consummating them. The important distinction is that his wound was physical and not psychological and that he was not emasculated.*[2]

The difference between Jake Barnes's wound and Hemingway's is adumbrated by a northern Michigan friend. This man, who does not wish to be identified, was told by Hemingway after the War about the wounds he had suffered in Italy. Besides being shot in the legs, Hemingway told his friend, he also was shot through the scrotum.

This, demonstrably, was not a permanently disabling wound, as Hemingway subsequently became the father of three boys. His sex life was not halted for long, if the unofficial accounts of his recuperation in Milan and his exploits of a year later in Michigan are accurate. The person who knew about Hemingway's war wounds added that in all of Ernest's Michigan relationships, "the women all seemed very satisfied. They all had nothing but good things to say about Ernie."

A nurse who had taken care of the Hemingway children told William Dawson in an interview that she "remembered Dr. Hemingway's telling her about the two hundred and thirty-seven pieces of shrapnel (*it was two hundred and twenty-seven*) in his son's groin and of the pain it caused him."[3] Although the two hundred and twenty-seven pieces of shrapnel were dispersed throughout his legs, the former nurse of the Hemingways raises the question of whether or not Ernest Hemingway also sustained a war injury in the groin.

Guy C. Conkle, M.D., who lives in Boyne City and

treated Hemingway, practices in the same second-story office that the young writer came to after World War I. Located on the main street of the small town, the office is reached by a narrow flight of stairs. The dark waiting room is usually filled.

The elderly doctor still remembers his patient. "Ernest was badly shell-shocked when he came for treatment in the summer of 1919. He was staying over at the Dilworths' [*in Horton Bay*], who rented rooms and cottages to lodgers. In October he moved up to Petoskey. Ernest had shrapnel in both of his legs. As a patient, he was brave but very nervous. He was a brilliant person and spoke about interesting things. Ernest was stout and was in good condition, except for his war wounds and their effects. He was always hunting and fishing."

To heal his wounds and to mend himself in every way, Hemingway returned to his beloved lake country for the summer of 1919 and remained for part of the winter. This was the gestation period for more of his Michigan stories.

Horton Bay

The sleepy little town of Horton Bay figured prominently in the early life of Ernest Hemingway and was the setting for one of his earliest stories, "Up in Michigan." Horton Bay remains much the same as when the young writer lived, loved, and was married there. Most of the white, frame houses still stand along the road leading from Boyne City to Charlevoix. Gone are the great elms along the main road, which is now paved, but the second-growth timber of the 1910's and early 1920's has now grown tall and verdant. The original road which Hemingway wrote about parallels the new highway. The Methodist Church and the Hortons' house have disappeared, but the general store and the Dilworth houses are standing. The sandy road still runs through the trees to the bay, and the bay is the same: deep blue, half encircled by the wooded point, and ringed with a narrow beach.

Although the story "Up in Michigan" was written by Hemingway in Paris in 1921, it depicts the small town of Horton Bay. The town has three spellings: "Horton Bay" on present maps and signs, "Horton's Bay" on pre-1904 maps, and "Hortons Bay" when used by Hemingway.

Carl Edgar, Hemingway's Kansas City–Horton Bay friend, commented on the condition of the young author when he came back from the war and lived in Horton

Bay. He thought that Hemingway was "figuratively and literally shot to pieces. He seemed to have a tremendous need to express the things that he had felt and seen."[1]

This expression took the form of stories past and present about northern Michigan and about the War in Italy. They were violent, painful stories which expressed Hemingway's mood of the time. Each was based in some way on his own experience, which he felt compelled to write about, and certainly none of them was full of love for his fellow man.

When Hemingway showed "Up in Michigan" to Gertrude Stein in Paris, she read it and said that no one would ever publish it, because it was too frank. Rejected by many magazines, it finally appeared in *Three Stories and Ten Poems* in 1923. This first book of Hemingway's was published by Robert McAlmon at the Contract Publishing Company of Paris and Dijon, and there were only three hundred copies printed. The book contained two other stories, "Out of Season" and "My Old Man," neither of which had a northern Michigan setting. Two years later "Up in Michigan" was not included in the Horace Liveright edition of *In Our Time*, probably for the reason that Gertrude Stein mentioned, but it was included in subsequent collections of Hemingway's short stories which were published by Charles Scribner's Sons.

"Up in Michigan" is about the seduction of a young country virgin, Liz Coates, by a virile blacksmith; the setting is Horton Bay. As mentioned before, Hemingway's parents owned a summer cottage on nearby Walloon Lake, and Hemingway, as a young man, spent a great deal of time at Horton Bay with a group of young people with whom he hunted, fished, and "pal'd around." In the fall of 1919, after his parents had returned to Oak Park at the end of the summer season, he stayed on at the home of the James Dilworths.

Horton Bay held many memories for Hemingway; it

was the home of his teenage friends, the place he chose to stay after his parents returned to Oak Park, and the village where he married Hadley Richardson. For his first published story with a Michigan background, it is obvious that Hemingway could not have chosen a village with which he was more familiar. Charles Fenton, when he was writing about northern Michigan wrote:

> *The area as a whole, as well as its associations and implications, gave Hemingway the material for a large part of his earliest published fiction. One of his first stories, "Up in Michigan," was drawn from it.*[2]

In this particular story Hemingway probably invented the plot, but he describes the setting of Horton Bay with photographic realism.

In the first paragraph of the story, the main character's name is Jim Gilmore, a man who had come to Horton Bay from Canada and bought the blacksmith shop from "old man Horton." "Old man Horton," as he is still called by the residents of Horton Bay, was the first settler of this little village on the small bay of the same name.

On the first of August, 1856, the only settlers of Pine River (Charlevoix), Medad Thompson and his family, saw a sail coming around the point from the direction of Little Traverse (Harbor Springs). The small sailboat headed for the mouth of the river with "a number of persons" on board. The boat was the "Rover" and carried, as passengers and crew, Samuel Horton and his family and two young men, John Newman and Archie Buttars.[3]

Samuel Horton, after stopping at Pine River, sailed down Lake Charlevoix to settle on the shores of the little bay which he named Horton's Bay after himself. At the beginning of the winter of 1856–57, Samuel Horton, his family, and Newman and Buttars comprised one of the four households in the Charlevoix region.

James Dilworth (Hemingway spelled the name "Dillworth" in his fiction), the owner of the house where Hemingway stayed in the autumn of 1919, was probably the inspiration for the character of Jim Gilmore, the blacksmith in the story. Dilworth owned the Horton Bay blacksmith shop and physically resembled the Jim Gilmore in the story, who was described as having had heavy eyebrows and a moustache and as standing about five feet, seven inches tall. After this description, in the first paragraph of the story, the fictional character departs from his real-life counterpart. James Dilworth neither lived over the blacksmith shop nor took his meals at the Smiths', as does Jim Gilmore, the fictional character.

Were the D. J. Smiths neighbors of the Dilworths? It is possible; at any rate, there were Smiths living in Horton Bay at the time, and to the best recollection of surviving neighbors, Smith's initials were D. J. Hemingway shared an apartment at 100 East Chicago Street in Chicago, during the winter and spring of 1921, with the older brother of his good friend, Bill Smith, who was always known as Y. K. Smith, practically never by his first name.

The real-life antecedents of the story's seduced virgin, if any, are not so easy to determine. Hemingway's sister, Marcelline, jumped to the conclusion that the "Liz Coates" of the story was inspired by Liz Dilworth, James Dilworth's wife, ignoring the physical dissimilarities between the two. Liz Dilworth was prematurely gray when Hemingway knew her and was otherwise unlike the fictional character. This did not soften Marcelline's shocked outrage at the story.

In her book she wrote:

> *The two main characters of the story, a man and a woman, had the same names as two of our family friends, a couple of whom we were particularly fond. The description of them in the tale, especially of the man, fitted our friends so accurately that as I read on*

*and realized that Ernest had put these kindly people
into this vulgar, sordid tale he had invented, my stom-
ach turned over. It wasn't just the story that affected
me, shocking as it was. It was Ernest's apparent lack of
any decent consideration for the people whose names
and detailed descriptions he had used in the story that
horrified me.*[4]

"Vulgar, sordid tale," "shocking," "decent consideration," and "horrified me" are the words his sister, who told
neighbors in Michigan that she was the one who understood her brother, used when she wrote about "Up in
Michigan." She was afraid that the Dilworth family might
run across a copy of the story and "be humiliated beyond
words." But the Dilworths were discerning enough to
realize how the young writer had constructed his story;
they recognized the description of Horton Bay, their
house, and the description of themselves. They knew that
the actions of the characters in the story were not meant to
be theirs and thought no more about it. Mrs. Wesley
Dilworth, James Dilworth's daughter-in-law was pleased,
not humiliated, and she was the one who identified all of
the characteristics of her in-laws which were used in this
chapter. Marcelline, like her parents, was unable to understand the artistic fact-fiction manipulation which her
brother used to construct a story. She was more concerned
with moral principles and her apprehensions of how the
Dilworths would accept the story, but the Dilworths had
more understanding of the creative process than she realized.

In "Up in Michigan" Hemingway gives an accurate
description of the town of Horton Bay. As he describes it
in the story, "Hortons Bay" was only five houses on the
main road between Boyne City and Charlevoix. Hemingway mentions the general store, which is still serving the
community with its "high false front," although now

automobiles stop there for gasoline, replacing the wagons "hitched out in front."

The five houses on the main road which runs through Horton Bay are named in the story with no attempt by the author at disguise. The Smith house is the first one that he mentions. According to their neighbors, these Smiths were from St. Louis. Ernest's friend, Bill Smith, did not stay with D. J. Smith of Horton Bay but with his aunt, Mrs. Charles, who owned a house and an orchard just outside of town.

The second house is identified as the "Strouds' house." All of the Strouds are now dead. Their house is across the street from the general store. The next house in the line is that of the Dilworths. The Dilworths owned the two houses on the side road that leads down to the bay, and the granddaughter of the James Dilworths now lives in one of the houses, "Pinehurst." This cottage is the probable setting for much of "Up in Michigan."

Next comes "Horton's house." This home of the original settlers was located on the main road leading out of town, but no longer stands. The "Van Hoosens" mentioned in the story are now also dead, but their son, Stanley Van Hoesen (the correct spelling of the name), lived in Boyne City in 1960 and worked at the Post Office there.

Hemingway wrote that the houses were "in a big grove of elm trees." Many large trees line either side of the main road, but the elm trees in Hemingway's story were destroyed in the elm blight which killed most of the trees in the Midwest. Hemingway then described the road as being "very sandy." It existed, and still does, but is no longer the main road, having been bypassed by a modern asphalt highway running parallel to it. Hemingway wrote in 1921 that "there was farming country and timber each way up the road."[5] This statement was true then and still is. Miles of fields and woods spread out at either end of the town.

Hemingway continued his word picture: "Up the road a ways was the Methodist Church and down the road in the other direction was the township school."[6] The Methodist Church was where he married Hadley Richardson. The church, a white, frame structure, was torn down about thirty years ago. The township school is still standing and has a New England flavor, as do many of the houses, schools, and churches in the area. The prim austerity of line is unsoftened, and the white paint heightens the angularity.

The blacksmith shop Hemingway describes was painted red and faced the school. The real shop is no longer standing, but the residents of Horton Bay say that it was indeed painted red, and it also was across the road from the school. In the next paragraph he writes about a "steep sandy road" that "ran down the hill to the bay through the timber."[7] The steep, sandy road still runs between the trees and underbrush and leads to the blue water of the bay. At night you can almost feel the presence of the drunken Jim and shy Liz, as they walked through the dark, the sand sliding out from beneath their feet. The view that is next described by Hemingway could not be seen clearly from Smith's cottage, but if Liz had stood at the back door of the Dilworth cottage, where Hemingway himself probably stood when he lived there, the following description would be photographically accurate:

> *From Smith's back door you could look out across the wood that ran down to the lake and across the bay. It was very beautiful in the spring and summer, the bay blue and bright and usually whitecaps on the lake out beyond the point from the breeze blowing from Charlevoix and Lake Michigan.*[8]

From the front lawn of the cottage next door one can see Lake Charlevoix, the bay, and the point across the woods. While Liz Coates looks at this view, in the story, she watches the ore barges on their way to Boyne City. The ore barges no longer travel across Lake Charlevoix to Boyne City, but there are many other boats which can still be watched "across the woods."

In the following paragraph Liz Coates continues to think about Jim Gilmore and his way of life. According to Mrs. Wesley Dilworth, James Dilworth "talked about the shop to D. J. Smith," as did "Jim Gilmore" in the story. When the season opened, Jim "took a wagon and tent, grub, axes . . . and went on a trip to the pine plains beyond Vanderbilt deer hunting."[9] During the fall he spent with the Dilworths, Hemingway did the same. Hemingway also used to fish "down east" which locally means across the Michigan peninsula below Vanderbilt. Wesley Dilworth, Kathryn Dilworth's deceased husband, went hunting and fishing with Hemingway and often said that he, not Doctor Hemingway, was the one who taught Ernest Hemingway to hunt and fish.

The story approaches its climax with a description of the returning hunters drinking and eating. Finally, Jim, feeling warm with liquor, makes tentative sexual advances towards Liz. Jim asks her to take a walk with him, and they walk down the sandy road towards the dock and the warehouse. (The warehouse and dock have since been torn down.) The seduction scene follows. The end of the story describes Liz Coates after Jim has fallen asleep on the dock. She walks across the dock, up the road to go to bed, as a cold mist comes through the woods from the bay.

Hemingway's descriptions are those of a reporter who saw the landscape accurately and without sentiment. About this particular story the following statement which Hemingway made later is pertinent:

Write about what you know and write truly and tell them where they can place it . . . all good books are alike in that they are truer than if they had really

*happened . . . the good and the bad, the ecstasy, the
remorse and sorrow, the people and the places and how
the weather was.*[10]

In "Up in Michigan" Hemingway wrote certainly
about what he knew and about "the people and the places
and how the weather was."

Marjorie and Bill

The characters "Marjorie" and "Bill" in "The End of Something" and "The Three-Day Blow" were patterned after a girl from Petoskey named Marjorie and a boy named Bill who summered in Horton Bay. The real Marjorie and Bill were Ernest Hemingway's best girl and best friend during the summer when the young author was nineteen, just as the fictional characters were Nick Adams's best girl and best friend in the story.

The fictional Marjorie and Bill, who have no last names in the stories, resemble the real-life Marjorie Bump and Bill Smith. Marjorie Bump used "Marj" as the short form of her name, although Hemingway spells the nickname of his fictional Marjorie as "Marge."

"The End of Something," which was first published in *In Our Time*, is the first Michigan love story which Hemingway handles from the male point of view. Because Hemingway understood and identified with the character of Nick, "The End of Something" is more poignant and sensitive than the brutal story "Up in Michigan." "The End of Somthing" is the story of the end of the love which Nick had for a girl named Marjorie. Nick takes her trolling for trout and later, when they sit by a campfire, he tells her to leave, perhaps for good.

Few of the critics seem to be interested in "The End of Something," except to agree that it is reminiscent of the love stories of F. Scott Fitzgerald. George Hemphill, in an article entitled "Hemingway and James," observes that this story fails

> *because no necessary connection (other than biographical, perhaps) between the end of the boy and girl affair between Nick and Marjorie and the end of the old lumbering days in Michigan is suggested.*[1]

He thinks that Hemingway should have "written it up" and

> *should make it a fine little tract with the message: The wages of acquisitiveness is death. Just as the lumber kings of Michigan at the end of the last century denuded the pine forests by overcutting, the young lovers killed their love by going ahead with it too fast.*[2]

Mr. Hemphill has an interesting idea, but Hemingway did not write or intend to say this in "The End of Something." All of Hemingway's titles are accurate and often explain or illuminate the story, and, in this case, he means what he says; this is a story about the end of a boy's love for a girl. If he also meant "The End of Something" is the end of Horton Bay as a lumbering town, Hemingway did not need to "write it up." The clarity and meaning of the story are contained in its present length.

When Mr. Hemphill writes that this story is biographical, he is nearer the truth. When he makes connections between the landscape and the characters, he again is sidetracked. Hemingway probably set the story in Horton Bay simply because that is where, without much doubt, the original action took place. His description of the town's past, and his selection of scenery, which he uses as a background, are important only in that they give the reader a sense of time and place. Hemingway wrote about what he knew, and in "The End of Something" he changed fact very little, except to heighten his story or conceal the identity of a character.

Doubt exists as to whether he ever meant to comment upon the denuding of the pine forests or whether his lovers killed their love "by going ahead with it too fast."[3] What Hemingway did write was a sad, realistic story about the end of love, set against the familiar Horton Bay on Lake Charlevoix.

The opening paragraph of "The End of Something" is an excellent example of Hemingway's ability to write clearly, accurately, and effectively in describing past action and capturing the nostalgia of a bygone era. In the opening topical sentence explaining that Horton Bay was a lumbering town in the past, Hemingway evokes the economic tragedy which occurred when there was no more timber to be cut. The lumber schooners had come into the bay and carried away everything that was movable, including all of the machinery in the mill. An 1890 tintype of the Stroud house in Horton Bay (mentioned in "Up in Michigan"), which is an exact visual example of Hemingway's literary description, was recently uncovered in a Michigan attic.

The tintype shows the Stroud house, the lumber mill, stacked lumber by the water, the bay and the point, and even a lumber schooner at dock. On the afternoon when the tintype was taken, the people, perched on the railing by their comfortable house posing for the photographer with the summer breeze blowing the lace curtains out of an upstairs window, had no way of knowing that the mill and their livelihood were doomed.

In a single paragraph in "The End of Something," Hemingway presents a capsule history of Horton Bay. Describing the town, he evokes the sound of the mill saws which reached everyone in the village; then he follows with the poignant sentence: "Then one year there were no more logs to make lumber."[4] The rest of the paragraph painfully itemizes everything which was loaded onto the lumber schooners. When the reader reaches the last item in the paragraph, the list of saws, the men who worked at the mill, the rollers, belts, and iron loaded on the schooner with the last load of lumber have all made a visual impression on his mind. The schooner is then described as filling her sails and moving out into the open lake, "carrying with it everything that had made the mill a mill and Hortons Bay [*Hemingway's spelling*] a town."[5] The next paragraph tersely lists what is left of the deserted mill which is surrounded by sawdust: a ruin in the swampy meadow by the shore of the bay.

The stage is set for the story of the supposedly hard-hearted boy and the unsuspecting girl. They enact their story against a ruin and a village left to become a ghost town. Even in a Charlevoix County Historical Society Program prepared in 1935, the history of the town of "Horton's Bay" (as spelled in the program) is treated briefly and without hope:

> *Horton's Bay named for Samuel Horton, its first settler, had a dock and one or two stores. Quite a trade in wood and bark was carried on there. The bay is exceptionally beautiful, and the settlement is upon one of the finest sites to be found anywhere, but it has not seemed to have the right geographical location for a village.*[6]

Hemingway lived this story during the late summer of 1919, after he returned from the War, and the time is set at ten years after the mill was deserted. According to Mrs. Dilworth, who lived in Horton Bay during this entire period, Hemingway was correct in writing that by 1919 all that was left of the mill was sawdust. She also added, "There were two mills and they were moved away before 1910, closer probably to 1895. They moved everything down to Boyne City which has lumber mills to this day."

When Hemingway wrote this story, he observed that after ten years nothing was left of the mill except its white limestone foundations, which showed amidst the second growth of trees as his lovers rowed past it. The "second growth" has since grown into a thick woods, and nothing remains of the mill's foundation. A small creek, which used to furnish some power to the mill, still runs clear and bubbling through the forest, and a small waterwheel turns on the spot where the large lumber mill used to stand. The creek's banks drop from shallows to deep water and have not changed since Hemingway described them in his short story.

The girl, Marjorie, who accompanies Nick in this story has caused quite a bit of controversy among the people in northern Michigan who knew Hemingway, because Hemingway himself went with a girl named Marjorie during the summer and fall of 1919, and the action of this story probably takes place in the late summer of 1919. Ernest Hemingway was a dashing young man at that time: a veteran who often wore his Italian uniform and was still using a cane.

The real girl, Marjorie Bump, was at that time about three years younger than Hemingway, which made her seventeen. She had red hair, dimples, and was described as being piquant, not beautiful or pretty. In the Petoskey High School yearbook her photograph reveals a pudgy, cute, smiling girl who looks young and vulnerable. Under her picture is the quotation, "It's the songs you sing and the smiles you wear that rush the sunshine everywhere." She was the Dramatics Editor in her senior year and was a member of the Charms, the Glee Club, and the Girls' Literary Society. The Literary Society at Petoskey High School in the 1920's held speaking events mainly of a social nature. Hemingway probably met Marjorie Bump in Horton Bay, where she spent her summers with her uncle, Ernest Ohle. She waited on tables at the Dilworths' when Hemingway was staying there.

Many residents of Petoskey remember the young Hemingway as "having a case on Marj." Some even speculate as to whether or not she was the reason he moved to Petoskey for the fall and part of the winter of 1919–20. Hazel Potter (daughter of the owners of the boarding house where Hemingway stayed in Petoskey) said that she never remembered him taking out anyone else when he lived in Petoskey.

In "The End of Something" Marjorie and Nick discuss the mill ruin, and Nick says that he can "just" remember when it was a mill. Marjorie is more romantic than Nick and refers to the mill as "our old ruin," which implies that they might have had some personal associations with the mill. She also thinks that it seems "more like a castle" than a mill. In the story they troll past the feeding trout and then head for the point. After they set out several lines, Marge, who is rowing, pulls on the oars, bringing the boat on the beach. She steps from the boat, and Nick pulls it up. They then make a driftwood fire. It is Marjorie who gets a blanket and spreads it on the sand.

A critic who writes that this story does not have a "point" has not read it carefully. What is told in this story is the final scene of a cumulative series of actions; we see the boy rejecting the girl after a relationship. Then a stronger relationship is shown as ending the boy-girl one; Bill comes to Nick. They had talked about what Nick had planned to do and obviously had even arranged to meet at a certain place on the beach to discuss it. The lovers' trysting place becomes nothing more than the prearranged meeting place of the boyish conspirators.

The cause of the male-female breakup is deep and part of the experience of the boy, Nick, who will soon become the "Hemingway hero." Nick has broken up with Marjorie on the advice of his friend Bill. He tells her that he "feels as if everything was gone to hell inside of me,"[7] and that love is not fun anymore. Nick feels bad as she rows away by herself. When Bill comes, they talk.

Although the fictional Marjorie did not know it, the end of her love affair was planned from the beginning of the story. Only at the end does the reader realize that no matter what Marge had done or said, she was to be disposed of, and, on cue, Bill would enter the stage.

Nick is troubled, unhappy, and not sure that he has done the right thing in following Bill's suggestion. He is very much like the young Hemingway at this time who was wounded both literally and figuratively in the War, was uncertain as to his future, and was probably feeling "as though everything had gone to hell inside."[8] Neither Nick nor the twenty-year-old Hemingway was capable at that time of taking on the responsibility of another human being until he first knew himself.

In "The Three-Day Blow," which is the companion piece of "The End of Something" and was published for the first time in *In Our Time*, Nick Adams is again the hero, and Bill also appears. They discuss Marjorie, and many ideas that were not fully developed in the previous story are expanded in this one.

When a resident of Petoskey was asked if Hemingway had had an affair with Marjorie Bump, she answered, "Marj didn't give Ernest the time of day. He was mad about her and made a fool of himself over her. Marj was very popular and from a nice, substantial family." A teacher from Petoskey High School remembers "Ernie always hanging around the auditorium waiting for Marj. Marj was protected, and there is no chance that he had an affair with her." In William F. Dawson's interview, he reports the conversation of a woman who told him that her family was furious when Hemingway published *In Our Time*, because "he took no pot shots at us, but my brother said he had no right to treat Marjorie like he did.

He told Ernie off when a lot of his other friends were afraid to."[9] When Bill's attitudes are expressed in this story, it is valuable to know the positive side of the real Marj's character and also to know this biographical background in the light of the story.

The Bill who appears in this story and in the previous one must have been drawn from Bill Smith. Bill Smith lived with his uncle and aunt, Doctor and Mrs. Charles, who lived near Horton Bay in the summers. He had a sister, Kate Smith (who later married John Dos Passos), and two brothers. Everyone who was interviewed said that Bill lived with his aunt and uncle during the summers, not with his father as the Bill in this story did. Harold Loeb in his book *the way it was* wrote:

> *When we got back to Paris in the Spring of '25, Bill Smith was already there. Hem had often spoken about Bill, with whom he had spent many happy summers. Bill was, as Hem put it, "one swell guy . . ." Bill was about my height, brown-haired, blue-eyed, with a small scar on his cheek and a small mustache. Despite his unobtrusive manner I quickly discovered that he had a wit, which expressed itself in cynical wisecracks and that he was loyal, discreet, and reliable.*[10]

The Bill in "The Three-Day Blow" has the same characteristics which Loeb ascribed to Bill Smith.

A Bill is also mentioned in a poem by Hemingway published in the autumn of 1924 in *Der Querschmitt*. It is titled, "The Soul of Spain (In the manner of Gertrude Stein)" and is about Bill and his father who would never sit with a Democrat. Bill feels that democracy must go and is "the shit." The conversation in "The Three-Day Blow" has language similar to that used in Hemingway's poem. Bill and his father are also linked in both the poem and the story.

Mrs. Paul Scott Mowrer, the first Mrs. Ernest Hemingway, wrote about Bill Smith in a recent letter: "As to Bill Smith—he and his brother, Y. K., and sister, Katherine, were from St. Louis, but Y. K. and Kate lived in Chicago when I met E. H. Their mother was not living; she was a sister of Mrs. Charles of St. Louis, who brought up and beautifully mothered those children. Dr. Charles was a well-known oculist. Bill lived with them and went north with them summers to Horton Bay. His father was a very learned scholar, teaching Greek *et al.* at Tulane University near New Orleans. Bill was a delightful personality, not easy to get at—a devoted friend of Ernest's all his life. He came to Paris and also went to Spain with us."

The setting of "The Three-Day Blow" must have been based on the Charles's place, which has since burned down. The neighbors said that it was a "California-style" house, and, from their directions, the exact footsteps that Nick took in the story can be followed.

In the first paragraph Hemingway opens his story with a description which fits the Charles property. The rain has stopped as Nick turns into the road like the one going through the Charles's orchard. The author describes the trees as having been picked, and the fall wind blowing in their bare branches. The first of the autumn storms was blowing in "The Three-Day Blow." The road to Bill's aunt's house leads through the orchard to the cottage on the top of the hill. In back of her house is the garage, the chicken coop, and the second-growth timber which covered the Horton Bay area.

Bill greets Nick in the story and the two stand together, looking out over the orchard, beyond the road, the lower fields, and the woods on the point to the lake. Since the wind is blowing down the lake, they can see surf breaking on Ten Mile point.

Bill then invites Nick inside, and Nick asks whether Bill's father is in. In "The Three-Day Blow" the boys drink Irish Whiskey, then Scotch, talk about baseball, fishing, and their fathers. The fictional Bill's father, who is a painter, drinks too much and gets "wild sometimes." Nick's father, who is a doctor, claims that he has never taken a drink in his life. Nick then confesses that his father also told him that he had missed a lot. Perhaps this is the reason that Nick, and the "Hemingway hero," enjoy drinking.

Giving an example of the dialogue at this point in the story, J. Kashkeen in his article, "Ernest Hemingway: A Tragedy of Craftsmanship," accuses Hemingway of clumsiness in this passage. He does not seem to realize that Hemingway is re-creating the dialogue of two drunken boys. Hemingway captures the essence of this particular experience in this story so accurately and artistically that it is one of the most humorous, pathetic, and accurate accounts ever written of the speech patterns and attitudes of American teen-age boys.

Bill's and Nick's conversation about baseball is a reflection of the young Hemingway's interest in the sport. The two boys in the story later discuss fishing, which they decide is a much finer sport than baseball. Nick says that there is no comparison between baseball and fishing, and wonders how they had ever begun talking about the subject. Bill answers that it was a mistake and that: "Baseball is a game for louts."[11]

Hemingway wrote about both fishing and baseball in his letters dated 1919-21. When he covered the subject of baseball, it was not as a participant, but as a baseball fan. Fishing was different. When he wrote of fishing and his fishing trips, he became excited and his writing became enthusiastic, sometimes lyrical.

In one letter Hemingway wrote about a baseball argument which he had with a friend named Deggie. The discussion was held in a Petoskey kitchen during the fall of 1920 and was about an incident which had occurred the previous fall (1919—the time of "The Three-Day

Blow"). Apparently Hemingway had placed a bet on "the Sox last fall," and Deggie told him that it had served him right to lose the bet. According to the related discussion in Hemingway's letter, the young writer had thought, when he made his bet, that the series was honest. Deggie taunted Hemingway by needling him about his loss and saying that he did not blame the Sox for selling the series. The conversation is reminiscent of that of the boys in "The Three-Day Blow," except that Hemingway felt an urge, which he suppressed, to give Deggie a good spanking.

After they decide in "The Three-Day Blow" to invite Chesterton and Walpole to go fishing with them at the 'Voix (Charlevoix), Bill tells Nick that he was smart "to bust off that Marge business." Bill talks about the disadvantages of marriage, of working to make enough money to get married, and he then advises Nick to "fall for them but don't let them ruin you."[12] Nick does not say anything, or else he agrees in one word, to Bill's long statements.

The fictional Bill then begins to attack Marge's family in order to further rationalize Nick's breakup with her. He reminds Nick of "her mother and the guy she married."[13] This particular line has been quoted and misquoted around Petoskey. Bill finally says, "Now she can marry somebody of her own sort and settle down and be happy."[14] (It is interesting to note here that Marj Bump supposedly married a dentist.) Bill then says, "You can't mix oil and water and you can't mix that sort of thing any more than if I'd marry Ida that works for Strattons."[15]

As Bill talks, Nick becomes more and more unhappy that he has lost Marge. He thinks of "how he had planned to stay in Charlevoix all winter so he could be near Marge."[16] Hemingway did stay in Petoskey one winter to be near Marjorie Bump. Nick realizes that his love affair is over, "like when the three-day blows come now and rip all the leaves off the trees."[17] Here is another example of an excellent and exact "Hemingway title" illuminated by the author.

At this point in the story, the Nick of "The Three-Day Blow" becomes a more sympathetic character than he was in "The End of Something." His abrupt and cruel ending of his relationship with Marge is understandable when the reader is able to see the pressure Bill was applying. Bill was holding out to Nick all the bachelor values of being free to do what you please, being able to get drunk, hunt, fish, and not have to work, and, at the same time, pointing out the evils of marriage, such as "working trying to get enough money to get married,"[18] getting a "fat married look,"[19] having "to marry the whole family,"[20] and having a mother- and father-in-law "around the house all the time."[21] Against persuasion such as this it is not surprising that Nick chose to dispose of Marjorie.

In "The Three-Day Blow," Nick, after heeding Bill's advice, felt unhappy about Marjorie. He only knew that he once had her; she was gone, and he had sent her away. He felt that it was his fault. His plans for going to Italy with Marjorie, and all of the plans they had made together were now shattered.

Then Bill makes the mistake of saying that Nick "might get back in it again."[22] Nick is happy, because he realizes that nothing is ever finished or lost. He plans to go into town on Saturday. He feels lighter, because he thinks there is "always a way out."[23] At this point in the story Nick is now able to be affirmative. He does not need to get drunk now, and he wants to go outside to shoot. When he is outside, he decides that "the Marge business was no longer tragic . . . the wind blew it out of his head. Still he could go into town Saturday night. It was a good thing to have in reserve."[24]

We know that Hemingway must have gone into town on Saturday night and that he continued to see Marj Bump for some time. Hemingway eventually broke up with

Marjorie Bump sometime in the winter of 1919–1920. But she must have kept on good terms with his family, because on July 30, 1920, Doctor Hemingway sent a letter to his wife in which he wrote: "I am glad that Ursula [*Hemingway's sister*] is having a few days at Marjorie Bumps [*sic*]. Hope she [*meaning Ursula*] will not see Ernest."[25]

Ursula Hemingway Jepson continued to keep in touch with her friend, Marjorie Bump. She recently wrote in a letter: "I was a contemporary of Marj and Pudge Bump's and of G. E. (for Grace Edith) Quinlan's . . . Her [*Marjorie Bump's*] sons-in-law, daughters, and son are prominent people in their own fields. We had her son as our guest in Honolulu when he was on leave from the Air Force during World War II."

The struggle between the "best friend" and the "best girl" for both Nick Adams and Ernest Hemingway was won by the "best friend." Bill seems to appear again as Bill Gorton in *The Sun Also Rises*, where the two characters (this time Jake Barnes is the hero) fish, get drunk, exchange literary jokes, and talk about women, specifically about Brett Ashley. The "best friend" also won Ernest Hemingway: two years after he broke up with Marj Bump, Hemingway married Hadley Richardson, who was a friend of Kate Smith's, Bill Smith's sister. Bill Smith was a witness at their wedding and continued to see the young Hemingways in Paris and Spain.

Two-Hearted Rivers

Two Two-Hearted Rivers exist: one in the Upper Peninsula of Michigan which runs into Lake Superior and one used as the title of Hemingway's short story, "Big Two-Hearted River." The river in his story is not the Two-Hearted at all, but the Fox.

"Big Two-Hearted River: Part I and II" has caused more comment than any other of the Michigan stories. The controversy started when Hemingway was first accused, by Dean Gauss in 1925, of "having written a story in which nothing happened." "Big Two-Hearted River" appeared first in *This Quarter* in Paris in May, 1925, and then was included in *In Our Time*.

If this story is read by itself, looking merely at what it says, we read about a lone fisherman's expedition after trout. He gets a sandwich and coffee in the railway station at St. Ignace, Michigan, on the Upper Peninsula, and then rides the train northwest to the town of Seney, which has been destroyed by fire. From there he hikes under a heavy pack over the burned ground until he reaches a rolling pine plain. After a nap in a grove of trees, he moves on to his campsite near the river. At the river he makes camp, eats, and sleeps. Finally, there is a detailed report of a morning's fishing downstream from the camp.

At the present, the town of Seney consists of a few houses, cabins, gas stations, and a motel on Highway M-

28. The railroad tracks still run beside the highway on the south side. Seney was once a wild logging town at the center of a white-pine forest, but the new forest of scrubby, second-growth pine is interrupted by stretches of swamp. Now Seney's income comes from the summer visitors, who pass through on their way north, and from a company which builds ready-made homes.

In "Big Two-Hearted River" Nick Adams walks down the railroad tracks to a bridge spanning the river where he watches the trout in the clear water. But Nick does not remember the name of the river, and nowhere in the content of the story is the name of the river given. Only the title misleads the reader into thinking that the river running through Seney is the Two-Hearted River. One critic took Hemingway's title literally and thought that Nick in less than a day had hiked the thirty or forty miles, as the crow flies, to the larger branch of the Two-Hearted River. But the statement which definitely associates the story "Big Two-Hearted River" and the Fox River came from Hemingway himself in a letter to his father on March 20, 1925, which was mentioned in his brother's book:

> Ernest also promised to try to get a copy of This Quarter for Father when it came out because he was sure he would like Big Two-Hearted River. He said the river was really the Fox above Seney.[1]

From the comments of the critics, we can see an increasing awareness of the true "point" of this story. In a review in the Nation in 1926, Allen Tate stressed Hemingway's nature-bias and praised "Big Two-Hearted River," saying it was the "most completely realized naturalistic fiction of the age."[2] When F. Scott Fitzgerald read this story, he did so with the "most breathless unwilling interest," since Conrad had first compelled him to look at the sea.[3] Malcolm Cowley evaluated this story in 1944 in his introduction to *The Portable Hemingway*. Did anyone recognize anything in this story except a fishing trip? Only Cowley thought that the fishing was "an escape from a nightmare or from realities that have become a nightmare."[4]

In a letter written on August 1, 1920, and mailed from Boyne City, Michigan, Hemingway wrote that in the morning he was going out on the Black River and then in a couple of weeks to Seney. Also in a poem, "Along With Youth," which was published in *Three Stories and Ten Poems* further evidence of the historical past is shown in the last lines which mention the burning of the hotel in Seney, Michigan.

The hotel that burned down in Seney was not the "Mansion House" Hemingway named in his story, but the old White House Hotel. The foundations of this hotel can still be found among the weeds. It is unlikely that Nick, standing on the tracks in 1919 or 1920, would have found Seney completely burned out and deserted. Hemingway probably reshuffled the dates of Seney's past to make a more symbolic postwar story. He also wrote about the thirteen saloons which had lined Seney's one street before the fire. In the eighties and nineties Seney had even more saloons, approximately twenty-two. In 1891 the town was completely burned out by a forest fire, was rebuilt, and partially burned again in 1895. At that time the logging companies had moved on, leaving the scorched earth and tree stumps behind. But Seney was never totally burned to the ground, as in Hemingway's story. In 1937 Phil Grondin's general store was "one of the few remaining landmarks of Seney."[5]

In another section of "Big Two-Hearted River," Hemingway refers to a man named "Hopkins" who taught him how to make coffee a special way. This reference is probably to Charlie Hopkins who was the assignment editor of the Kansas City *Star*'s morning edition, the *Times*. They became close friends when Hemingway was working for the *Star*, and Hopkins went with Hemingway to northern Michigan on his last fishing trip before the war.[6] In this story Nick thinks of Hopkins as the water for the coffee boils. He remembers a fishing trip on the Black River when Hopkins left the fishing party after he received a telegram with the news of his first successful oil well. Nick also remembers that he never saw Hopkins again, and it had been a long time ago on the Black River. Hopkins gave his camera to Bill to remember him by. Bill of the "Big Two-Hearted River" is probably Bill Smith, Hemingway's fishing companion and close friend. When Hemingway wrote that Nick and Bill had never seen Hopkins again, this parallels the fact that in real life when he, Bill Smith, and Charlie Hopkins had fished before World War I, they also received a telegram in the north woods, but to call them to duty, not with the news of an oil well, and Hopkins might not have come back from the war. Nick and Hemingway had both fought and been injured in the war since the fishing trip with Hopkins. The remembrance of the lighthearted fishing trip on the Black River before the War throws into sharper contrast the therapeutic fishing trip of the war-torn man in "Big Two-Hearted River."

On August 15, 1924, Hemingway wrote to Gertrude Stein about what must have been the "Big Two-Hearted River" story:

> . . . *the long one I worked on before I went to Spain where I'm trying to do the country like Cezanne and having a hell of a time and sometimes getting a little bit. It is about 100 pages long and nothing happens and the country is swell, I made it all up, so I see it all and part of it comes out the way it ought to, it is swell about the fish, but isn't writing a hard job though?*[7]

Above: Horton Bay and point. "Marjorie stepped out of the boat and Nick pulled the boat high up the beach."—"The End of Something." *Below:* Horton Bay shoreline. "They made a fire of driftwood."—"The End of Something."

Above: Petoskey Public Library. "He had gone to the Public Library and asked for a book the night before."—*The Torrents of Spring. Below:* Petoskey. Potter's Rooming House at 602 State Street where Hemingway lived in the fall and winter of 1919–20.

Above: "Grace cottage" at "Longfield," Walloon Lake. This cottage was an issue in Ernest's twenty-first birthday argument with his mother. The Hemingway family no longer owns it, and its appearance has been altered since Ernest's days in Michigan. *Below:* Horton Bay. Looking toward Lake Charlevoix from the orchard on what was once the Charleses' property. "The rain stopped as Nick turned into the road that went up through the orchard. . . . It was the first of the autumn storms."—"The Three-Day Blow."

Social Items

The engagement of Miss Hadley Richardson, daughter of the late Mrs. Florence Wayman Richardson, to Ernest Miller Hemmingway of Chicago was announced yesterday at a tea with which Mrs. George J. Breaker of 5227 Westminster place entertained at her home. The wedding probably will take place in the fall. Miss Richardson is the sister of Mrs. Roland G. Usher. She received her education at Mary Institute and Bryn Mawr, and made an informal debut a few years ago. Mr. Hemmingway is the son of Dr. and Mrs. C. E. Hemmingway of Oak Park, Ill., and served with the Ambulance Corps during the war, and later attended the University of Padua in Italy. He was the first American to be wounded in Italy and was decorated by the King.

Left: The Richardson-Hemingway engagement announcement from a St. Louis newspaper saved by Hadley. *Below:* "Shangri-La," the Dilworth house in Horton Bay where the Richardson-Hemingway wedding reception was held. *Opposite page:* Hadley Richardson in her wedding dress, taken in St. Louis before her September 3, 1921, marriage to Ernest Hemingway.

Above: Little Traverse Bay as seen by Yogi Johnson: "On his right was a field that stretched to Little Traverse Bay. The blue of the bay opening out into the big Lake Michigan. Across the pine hills behind Harbor Springs. Beyond, where you could not see, Cross Village, where the Indians lived.—*The Torrents of Spring. Below:* A winter view of Petoskey taken in the 1890's.

Above: A nineteenth-century etching of Charlevoix, and its harbor, with Lake Charlevoix (then Pine Lake) in the distance. *Below:* An 1890's tintype of the Charlevoix harbor with lumber schooners and steamboats at dock.

A photograph of Ernest Hemingway taken in front of Grace Quinlan's house in the winter of 1920. Still using a cane, Hemingway was leaving for Toronto with a bottle of wine tucked into his coatpocket.

"*. . . isn't writing a hard job though?*" The young Hemingway, under the influence of Gertrude Stein, was learning that a writer must create rather than merely report. Miss Stein felt that journalism was detrimental to a young writer, not only because it encouraged him to report rather than make, but also because it weakened the writer through an artificial support. She believed that this support was the artificial sense of immediacy through which a newspaper story must create the illusion that the incident written about occurred at the same time the reader reads it. Obviously this is impossible. Hemingway realized in 1924 that journalistic immediacy was not a genuine immediacy.

In December, 1923, Hemingway resigned from the Toronto *Star Weekly*, and in January of 1924 he returned to Europe. "Big Two-Hearted River," which was written between January and August of 1924, is the piece of writing which announces the transformation of Hemingway the newspaperman into Ernest Hemingway, the creative writer.

Four years before writing this story, Hemingway wrote a series of articles for the Toronto *Star Weekly* drawn from his then recent fishing experiences. The following comparisons of his newspaper writing placed next to sections of "Big Two-Hearted River" show how he had matured from a reporter to a fiction writer.

The Toronto Star Weekly	*Big Two-Hearted River*
1. A high pine covered bluff that rises steep up out of the shadows. A short sand slope down to the river and a quick elbow turn with a little flood wood jammed in the bend and then a pool. (August 28, 1920)	1. He turned and looked down the stream. It stretched away, pebbly-bottomed with shallows and big boulders and a deep pool as it curved away around the foot of a bluff.[8]
2. The action is supplied by two figures that slog into the picture up the trail along the river bank	2. Nick slipped off his pack and lay in the shade. . . . His pack was heavy and the straps painful

The Toronto Star Weekly	Big Two-Hearted River
with loads on their backs that would tire a pack horse. These loads are pitched over the heads onto the patch of ferns by the edge of the deep pool. That is incorrect. Really the figures lurch a little forward and the top line loosens and the pack slumps on to the ground. Men don't pitch loads at the end of an eight mile hike. (August 28, 1920)	as he lifted it on. He leaned over with the pack on and picked up the leather rodcase and started out from the pine trees across the sweet fern swale, toward the river.[9]
3. The other is lying on his back and looking straight up in the air. (August 28, 1920)	3. He lay on his back and looked up into the pine trees. His neck and back and the small of his neck rested as he stretched. The earth felt good against his back. He looked up at the sky, through the branches, and then shut his eyes.[10]
4. We retired into our tent and dropped the mosquito netting over the front. Pretty soon a mosquito bit me on the nose. We cleared the tent of them and lay down to sleep and then came that familiar zoom and another proboscis was inserted into my face. The mosquitos were coming through the netting as though it were the bars of a cage . . . The moral is that we should have had cheesecloth instead of the kind of mosquito netting they are selling this year. (August 5, 1920)	4. Across the open mouth of the tent Nick fixed cheesecloth to keep out mosquitos. He crawled under the mosquito bar with various things from the pack to put at the head of the bed under the slant of the canvas. It smelled pleasantly, of canvas. Already there was something mysterious and homelike.[11]
5. The stew kettle will cook you dried apricots when they have resumed their pre-dried plumpness after a night of soaking, it will serve to concoct a mulligan in, and it will cook macaroni. When you are not	5. While he waited for the coffee to boil, he opened a small can of apricots. He liked to open cans. He emptied the can of apricots out into a tin cup. While he watched the coffee on the fire, he drank the juice syrup of the

The Toronto Star Weekly

Big Two-Hearted River

using it, it should be boiling water for the dishes.
(June 26, 1920)

apricots, carefully at first to keep them from spilling, then meditatively, sucking the apricots down. They were better than fresh apricots.[12]

6. By smearing ourselves with citronella oil we managed to get some sleep. About as much sleep as a man gets with a few thousand buzzing, biting, ungentlemanly insects settling down on his face as soon as it comes out of the blankets and satisfying their hunger by pushing their bills into his countenance.
(August 5, 1920)

6. Nick stretched under the blanket comfortably. A mosquito hummed close to his ear. Nick sat up and lit a match. The mosquito was on the canvas, over his head. Nick moved the match quickly up to it. The mosquito made a satisfactory hiss in the flame. The match went out. Nick lay down again under the blanket.[13]

7. The big difficulty about fishing with grasshoppers has always been the difficulty in catching them. The classic way is to get up early in the morning before the sun has dried the dew, and catch the hoppers while they are still stiff and cold and unable to hop more than a feeble foot or two. They are found under the side of logs in a clearing and along the grass stems.
(April 24, 1920)

7. The meadow was wet with dew and Nick wanted to catch grasshoppers for bait before the sun dried the grass. He found plenty of good grasshoppers. They were at the base of the grass stems. Sometimes they clung to a grass stem. They were cold and wet with the dew, and could not jump until the sun warmed them. Nick picked them up, taking only the medium-sized ones, and put them into the bottle. He turned over a log and just under the shelter of the edge were several hundred hoppers. It was a grasshopper lodging house.[14]

8. With the prepared pancake flours you take a cup full of pancake flour and add a cup of water. Mix the water and flour and as soon as the lumps are out it is ready for cooking. Have the skillet hot and keep it well greased. Drop the batter in and

8. Rapidly he mixed some buckwheat flour with water and stirred it smooth, one cup of flour, one cup of water. He put a handful of coffee in the pot and dipped a lump of grease out of a can and slid it sputtering across the hot skillet. On the smoking

The Toronto Star Weekly | *Big Two-Hearted River*

as soon as it is done on one side loosen it in the skillet and flip it over. Apple butter, syrup or cinnamon and sugar go well with the cakes.
(June 26, 1920)

skillet he poured smoothly the buckwheat batter. It spread like lava, the grease spitting sharply. Around the edges the buckwheat cake began to firm, then brown, then crisp. The surface was bubbling slowly to porousness. Nick pushed under the browned under surface with a fresh pine chip. He shook the skillet sideways and the cake was loose on the surface. I won't try and flop it, he thought. He slid the chip of clean wood all the way under the cake, and flopped it over onto its face. It sputtered in the pan . . . Nick ate a big flapjack and a smaller one, covered with apple butter.[15]

9. Trout rise to a hopper far more readily than they do to a fly, and they are bigger trout. If you want to insure catching big trout, put three good sized hoppers on the hook. Put the hook in under the chin of the grasshopper and carry it back through the thorax. A triple hopper bait is too large for the smaller trout to hit, and tempts the old whangle berries.
(April 24, 1920)

9. Another hopper poked his face out of the bottle. His antennae wavered. He was getting his front legs out of the bottle to jump. Nick took him by the head and held him while he threaded the slim hook under his chin, down through his thorax and into the last segments of his abdomen. The grasshopper took hold of the hook with his front feet, spitting tobacco juice on it. Nick dropped him into the water.[16]

10. We were fishing for rainbow trout where a little river comes into a lake and cuts a channel alongside the bank. Into the mouth of this river and the bay it empties out of the big lake. They chase the shiners and young herring and you can see their back fins coming out of the water like porpoises with a shower of minnows shooting up into the air.

10. There was a long tug. Nick struck and the rod came alive and dangerous, bent double, the line tightening, coming out of water, tightening, all in a heavy, dangerous, steady pull. Nick felt the moment when the leader would break if the strain increased and let the line go.

The reel ratched into a mechanical shriek as the line went

The Toronto Star Weekly   *Big Two-Hearted River*

Every once in a while a big trout will jump clear of the water with a noise like somebody throwing a bathtub into the lake. . . .

None of these lake rainbows run under four pounds and when one hits the minnow the reel buzzes, the rod tip jerks down and you grab the rod and strike and the fight is on. The point of this is that we have caught trout in this over nine pounds in weight. We have never had one run out all the line and while we have lost many leaders we had never had a fish big enough to break the line.

One day in September I had just cast out the minnow into the channel, the rod was pointing up into the air and the click was set on the reel. I was about twenty-five yards down the shore getting some driftwood for a fire when the reel gave a shriek that mounted to about a high C. Not the familiar bzzzzzzzz but a steady shriek. The rod jerked down so hard that it flattened straight out on the water.

I raced for the rod the instant I heard the reel start. Just as I reached it the shriek of the reel stopped. There was a big wallowing explosion out on the lake, the line broke at the reel and the rod, the butt had been under a log and resting on another, shot up into the air. I jumped into the water but the line had vanished out into the lake.

Don't ask me how big he was.

out in a rush. Too fast. Nick could not check it, the line rushing out, the reel note rising as the line ran out.

With the core of the reel showing, his feeling stopped with the excitement, leaning back against the current that mounted icily his thighs, Nick thumbed the reel hard with his left hand. It was awkward getting his thumb inside the fly reel frame.

As he put on pressure the line tightened into sudden hardness and beyond the logs a huge trout went high out of water. As he jumped, Nick lowered the tip of the rod. But he felt, as he dropped the tip to ease the strain, the moment when the strain was too great; the hardness too tight. Of course, the leader had broken. There was no mistaking the feeling when all spring left the line and it became dry and hard. Then it went slack.

His mouth went dry, his heart down, Nick reeled in. He had never seen so big a trout. There was a heaviness, a power not to be held, and then the bulk of him, as he jumped. He looked as broad as a salmon. . . .

The leader had broken where the hook was tied to it. Nick took it into his hand. He thought of the trout somewhere on the bottom, holding himself steady over the gravel, far down below the light, under the logs, with the hook in his jaw. Nick knew the trout's teeth would cut through the snell of the hook. The hook would imbed itself in his jaw.

The Toronto Star Weekly	*Big Two-Hearted River*
But he was big enough to break a brand new twenty-three-pound test line without an instant's strain. As soon as his weight hit the direct pull of the line it snapped. (November 20, 1920)	He'd bet the trout was angry. That was a trout. He had been solidly hooked. Solid as a rock. He felt like a rock, too, before he started off. By God, he was a big one. By God, he was the biggest one I ever heard of.[17]

Hemingway's accurate descriptions when he catalogues the physical characteristics of the landscape are sharper and more mature than the rest of his newspaper work. Although the narrative and expository gifts of the Toronto *Star Weekly* reporter are not to be belittled as the work of a twenty-year-old, the contrasting excellence of his fiction written only four years later shows how seriously he took Gertrude Stein's suggestions. When he wrote to her in 1924 discussing the work he was doing, he said, "[*Writing*] used to be easy until I met you."[18]

The language of Hemingway's true reportorial style, not the style that some critics claim to find in his fictional works, is evidenced in the above quotations from the Toronto *Star Weekly*. In his transference of experience into fiction, Ernest Hemingway evoked every physical sensation through an accurate, yet artistically contrived account of the experience, so that his fictionalized account is more real to the reader than his reportorial account.

In "Big Two-Hearted River" Nick fishes in the same place Hemingway had written about in his letter. He experiences the same attitudes and sensations Hemingway wrote about in the newspaper excerpts. Nick remembers the same people and events Hemingway remembered, such as Charlie Hopkins and the burning of the Seney hotel. The logical conclusion is that this story is probably a lesson in the writing of fiction drawn very accurately from a fishing trip Hemingway took on the Fox River in the summer of 1919 or 1920.

Petoskey

The fall of 1919 and the winter of 1920, when Hemingway lived in Petoskey, were important to him, both as a person and as a writer. Able to be independent from his family physically and emotionally, he had the time to begin writing seriously. The solitary time writing gave him a chance to assess his war experience and gain a perspective about his own life and drives.

Ernest at twenty was regarded as a problem by his parents. As a product of an educated, upper-middle-class family, Hemingway must also have had some doubts about himself. The college education expected of a doctor's son and of the product of a family with a tradition and respect for education had been missed by the doctor's eldest son.

At twenty, with the maturing experiences of a job on the Kansas City *Star* and the War behind him, Hemingway was considered ready for a job, but too old to enter college. The lack of a college education sometimes later bothered him, but it did not hamper his desire for his sons' college educations or his own lifelong self-education through extensive reading. The possibility exists that if Hemingway had gone to college for four years, he would not have had the time to evolve his personal writing style gained from his early newspaper experience and his own persistent experiments with words. Not hampered by his lack of a formal college education, he published his first book, *Three Stories and Ten Poems*, at twenty-four, when most college graduates were just getting settled in their first jobs, and at thirty he was world famous as the author of *The Sun Also Rises* and *A Farewell to Arms*.

After an early autumn spent in Horton Bay, Hemingway moved to Petoskey when the weather grew colder, probably to be near Marj Bump. He took a room with the Potters, who lived at 602 State Street and took in boarders. Their daughter, Hazel Potter, still recalls the boarder who lived in the front room during the fall and winter of 1919–1920. She was working in Mancelona at the time, but returned to Petoskey on weekends.

This is the same Miss Potter who remembered that Marjorie Bump was the only girl Hemingway ever took out. Miss Potter also remembers the boarder as being "big and dark," and that he was "typing away all the time."

Many of the staid citizens of Petoskey disapproved of the way Hemingway looked and dressed when he lived among them. Fond of "roughing it," Hemingway often wore old shoes and pants with a Mackinaw shirt and topped it off with several days' beard. He also "ran around with a wild gang and drank heavily during prohibition," according to some members of the established families of Petoskey.

Many of the churchgoing, straitlaced families held a low opinion of the boy from Chicago who lived at the Potters', not working, and not conforming to their ideas of dress and conduct. But the ladies of the town "turned out" to hear his speech about his war experiences. The talk was held at the public library, which still stands, and was for the benefit of the Arts Study Group of the Ladies' Aid Society. For the lecture the handsome ex-soldier dressed in the uniform of the Italian Army and slung over his shoulders a long, black cape with a velvet collar. He told the ladies that, when he was lying at the evacuation point after he had been wounded, "it seemed more reasonable to die than to live."

Hemingway was learning how to live again in Petoskey, and fortunately he had many good friends who did not share the opinions of the more conservative members of the town. One of his close friends was Grace Quinlan, who later married Joseph E. Otis, junior, and lived in South Bend, Indiana, but spent her summers near Harbor Springs. She died in 1964, but in 1960 discussed in an interview her friendship with Hemingway.

Mrs. Otis was an attractive woman with blue-black hair, which she wore pulled into a bun at the back of her neck. Intelligent and perceptive, Mrs. Otis remembered well and kept all of the letters and mementos of her acquaintance with the young man who stayed after the other summer-resorters left. She was only fourteen when Ernest was nineteen, but the age difference did not hamper their friendship in Petoskey or their exchange of letters when she was at camp or Hemingway was in Chicago.

Mrs. Otis remembered Ernest Hemingway as being "very dashing, limping, and always telling stories which he was writing." She once went to a dance with him, but he was such a "terrible dancer we spent most of the evening sitting and talking." Hemingway came frequently to the Quinlans' house. According to Mrs. Otis, Marj Bump would also come over, and they would all sit around in the kitchen or the parlor and pop popcorn, listen to records, and talk. "Stein" was Hemingway's nickname then, and Mrs. Otis thought he gained it because "he drank so much beer out of a stein during the war." But the nickname "Stein," one of many Hemingway was to have, had a pre-World War I origin. When he was in high school, a group of his friends organized a bogus anti-prohibition political party and their slogan was "Hemingway and a full Stein!"

Another good friend of Hemingway's was E. G.

("Dutch") Pailthorp who was a judge's son and is presently a lawyer in his hometown, Petoskey. Pailthorp said that he and Hemingway and a group of their friends used to "hang out" at the Park House, a bar in the old Park Hotel which has since been torn down. George O'Neil (the name is similar to that of the main character of *The Torrents of Spring,* "Scripps O'Neil") was Hemingway's best friend, according to Pailthorp. George O'Neil left Petoskey, and the people there have lost touch with him.

"Dutch" Pailthorp, who is a large, redheaded man with an outgoing nature, recalled that his friend's room at the Potters' was neat and that there was a typewriter on a desk. Pailthorp confirmed that Hemingway was always writing, but all he received were rejection slips. When Hemingway was living in the boarding house, he did no other work aside from his writing. Pailthorp felt that he was "living off his Army pay, because he was financially independent. People had Ernie to dinner, but he wasn't a sponge."

Pailthorp said that Hemingway was a "man's man plus being a great sportsman." He remembered some incidents which probably helped to give Hemingway his "wild reputation" in Petoskey. One night Dutch and Ernest were in Hemingway's room at the Potters' drinking "home brew," which they made from cider, with raisins and cracked corn added. A religious sect had announced that the world was going to end that night, and the two young men decided they would die drunk. They spent the entire night drinking and when they woke up the next morning with hangovers, they wished that the world *had* ended.

Pailthorp recalled that on another night Ernest's friends had a "wild party" at Doctor Ramsdell's house in Bay View near Petoskey. According to Pailthorp, "we all drank our home brew and threw the raisins out the back door. When 'Doc' Ramsdell, senior, came over the next morning, he found all of the raisins in the back yard and couldn't figure out what happened."

Pailthorp also said that Hemingway was always telling him the stories he was writing. One of them was either never written or lost, but Pailthorp was able to remember it. Here is the story as Hemingway told it to Pailthorp in 1920 and as Pailthorp retold it in 1960:

"A wounded soldier was sent to the south of Italy on leave. On the way he met an Italian noblewoman who invited him to her villa. Since the soldier was just going to rest camp, he accepted. They slept together that night. The next morning when they are having breakfast, her husband walks in and catches them together.

"The husband challenges the soldier to a duel and offers him his choice of weapons. The soldier says that he will duel in the American fashion. The Italian asks him what that will be. He answers by saying, 'In America we use pistols. Now you stand at one end of the breakfast table, and I will stand at the other end. Your wife will stand between us and count to three. At the count of three we will both turn around and fire.' 'From the ends of the table?' asked the Italian. 'That's right,' answers the soldier. The husband is uncertain as to what to do, and at that moment the wife takes advantage of the opportunity to soften up her husband.

"The soldier slips upstairs and packs. As he is leaving, he passes the husband and wife, who are in an embrace by the breakfast table. The husband's back is to the soldier, but the wife is facing him. As the soldier sneaks out of the door, the wife winks at him behind her husband's back."

Hemingway also told Pailthorp that when "he enlisted in the Army, he wanted to fly airplanes, but couldn't do that, so he enlisted in the ambulance corps of the Italian Army." Hemingway told Pailthorp that the men he was fighting with were prisoners who had been freed to fight in the Italian Army and were a "rough crew." They would bind together the hands of two, Austrian prisoners in a square, tie them, place a hand grenade in the center, and blow up the two Austrians. According to Pailthorp, Hemingway also told about the Italian soldiers fighting with a knife clamped between their teeth. One night when all of the group was in "Doc" Ramsdell's barn in Petoskey, Hemingway threw a knife, the way the Italians had taught him, from across the barn and hit the exact crack in the wall at which he was aiming.

During the same winter Mr. Ralph Connable from Petoskey offered Hemingway a job tutoring his son at the Connables' winter home in Toronto. Connable was for many years head of the F. W. Woolworth chain in Canada and was an old friend of the Hemingway family. While in Toronto Connable introduced Hemingway to the feature editor of the Toronto *Star Weekly*, which resulted in the young newspaperman's four-year association with the *Star Weekly* and its parent paper, the *Daily Star*.

The time Hemingway spent in Petoskey was important to him, because he was unconsciously collecting facts and gaining a feel of the place. He later used Petoskey as the setting for his first published novel, *The Torrents of Spring*. But his first published novel was not the first novel he had written. Hemingway wrote *The Torrents of Spring* in ten days in November, 1925, after he had finished the first draft of *The Sun Also Rises*. Not bothering to polish *Torrents*, a neglect that was unusual for Hemingway, he sent it off to Boni and Liveright, who had an option on his "first novel."

Many people have speculated that Hemingway wrote *The Torrents of Spring* as a deliberate satire of Liveright's best sellers by Sherwood Anderson, in order to get out of his commitment to the publishers. F. Scott Fitzgerald had told Hemingway about Scribner's and, especially, about

Maxwell Perkins. Ernest had even written to Perkins promising him that he would give the editor the first chance to look at any new book in the event of a release from Liveright.

The first Mrs. Hemingway, Hadley, remembered the writing of *The Torrents of Spring* and, in a private interview, clarified what happened. "Ernest had talked to Scott about Scribner's and wanted to go there. He had a commitment to Liveright and wanted to get out of it, so he wrote *The Torrents of Spring* satirizing their top author, Anderson. I know that Ernest didn't really want to write the book in order to change publishers, but Pauline wanted him to do it, and so he did."

Sherwood Anderson was hurt by Hemingway's broad satire of his books, especially of his *Dark Laughter*, and called *Torrents* a "parodistic book which might have been humorous had Max Beerbohm condensed it to twelve pages."[1] After reading *Torrents*, Anderson must have regretted having had Horace Liveright send Hemingway a copy of *Dark Laughter* on August 28, 1925. The parody of Sherwood Anderson was so obvious and broad that when even the first paragraphs of *Dark Laughter* and *The Torrents of Spring* are read one after the other, their similarities are unmistakable. The character of Yogi Johnson of *Torrents* parallels that of Bruce Dudley of *Laughter*, while Hemingway's Scripps O'Neil is like Anderson's Sponge Martin.

Hemingway's pump factory in Petoskey recalls Anderson's wheel factory in Old Harbor, Indiana; both are located in the Midwest. The description of spring coming in Anderson's book afforded Hemingway a chance for poking fun with a changeable chinook wind heralding spring. The Negro laugh of Anderson is usually an Indian war whoop at the end of Hemingway's chapters, but becomes the laugh of a Negro at the end of Chapter XII.

Hemingway satirizes Anderson in other ways throughout his novel. He uses questions, as Anderson did, and has his characters view strange happenings filled with supposedly symbolic meaning. Hemingway makes lists of authors and mentions friends in the name-dropping manner of Anderson. And at the end of *Torrents* Yogi Johnson walks away from the town on the railroad tracks as do characters in many of Anderson's books. The main targets of Hemingway's novel were Sherwood Anderson's repeated peculiarities and tricks of style and his characters' naïve sexual promiscuity, pseudo philosophy, chaotic wanderings, and aimless self-mystification.

The similarities between *Dark Laughter* and *The Torrents of Spring* were so numerous that some of the other targets in Hemingway's book can be overlooked. His other literary targets included Gertrude Stein, James Joyce, Mencken, and possibly Dos Passos and D. H. Lawrence.

Hemingway must have read *Joseph Andrews* by Henry Fielding just before writing *The Torrents of Spring*. All of the quotations from Fielding which are used throughout *Torrents* are from one source: the "Author's Preface" of *Joseph Andrews*. Not only did Hemingway pick up mannerisms and style patterns from *Joseph Andrews*, but he organized *Torrents* in the same pattern of short chapters and division into sections headed Part I, II, III, and IV, while Fielding divided his *Joseph Andrews* into four "books." The young writer also gave summary chapter headings ("Red and Black Laughter," etc.) at the beginning of each part.

Hemingway's respect for Fielding earned him an enthusiastic review by Allen Tate who wrote in the *Nation* that Hemingway is "the best contemporary writer of the eighteenth-century prose" and that he had "written a novel which is on its own account, irrespective of momentary aim, a small masterpiece of American fiction."[2]

The Torrents of Spring is not a masterpiece, whether large or small, when compared to his other works, and the deflating of the Anderson balloon no longer seems important to contemporary readers. What does remain, though, in *Torrents* to make it worth reading now are its sections of broad humor and its ironic passages. Hemingway could be as clever and as literary as anyone when he needed to be, but he knew that he had more important books to polish and write and more important statements to make.

The title of the novel came from Turgenev (as with the story "Fathers and Sons"), but not the content. The content could only have come from Hemingway, with his knowledge of Petoskey, Anderson, and the literary talk and people of Paris in the twenties. The plot is a relatively unimportant tangle. Scripps O'Neil, a Harvard esthete, and Yogi Johnson, a World War I veteran of Swedish descent, work in a pump factory. Scripps, deserted by his first wife in Mancelona, has an Andersonian marriage with Diana, the senior waitress in Brown's Beanery. But Scripps is soon fascinated with Mandy, a younger waitress, who relates literary anecdotes. Diana tries to fight back by reading everything from *The New York Times Book Review* to *Harper's* but loses her man to the superior literary interest of Mandy's tales. Yogi Johnson finally goes back to nature by taking off his clothes as he accompanies a naked Indian squaw out of town on the railroad tracks.

The atmosphere of Petoskey and actual landmarks around the town are found throughout *Torrents*. Joe Bacon is sure that Hemingway "got his inspiration" for the book when Ernest and Bacon's son, Earl, walked along the railroad tracks to Petoskey one March day. They had to walk by the Blackmer Rotary Pump Company, and the water, at that point, rushed down the hillside until it covered the boys' knees. Hemingway had again described the places so accurately that they can be identified. Although Joseph Bacon knew nothing of Turgenev, he had read Hemingway's *Torrents* and recognized the pump factory (unnamed in the book) and the G.R. & I. railroad tracks leading out of Petoskey.

The town of Mancelona, a place the young train rider from Oak Park had passed through many times, is mentioned again. The Boyne Falls grade of the railroad track, similar to the grade in "The Battler," appears again. Scripps ends his beginning odyssey at the Petoskey railway station, which is no longer in use, but still has the large sign with PETOSKEY on it which Scripps observed.

McCarthy's Barber Shop, where, in the novel, two Indians received a shave while Scripps O'Neil watched through the window, is now only half as large as it was in Hemingway's day. McCarthy is no longer alive, and Braun's Restaurant in Petoskey, which sounds similar to "Brown's Beanery, The Best by Test," is gone.

In Chapter VI O'Neil walked from the beanery, past the barber shop, and turned onto the main street of Petoskey. He found that "It was a handsome, broad street, lined on either side with brick and pressed-stone buildings."[3] The main street is much the same, with a few of the buildings concealing their brick and pressed stone under post-World War II façades. Scripps later watched "the sunset out over the Petoskey Harbor, the lake now frozen and great blocks of ice jutting over the breakwater . . ."[4] A breakwater was necessary in the early twenties, and still is, to protect the harbor from the weather which comes straight off Lake Michigan. Although the Petoskey harbor is man-made and can only shelter small boats, it remains the best vantage point for a view of the sunset over the bay and its surrounding hills.

The longest description of the town and environs comes in Chapter XI, when Yogi Johnson leaves the pump factory and takes a short walk out of town. He first crosses the bridge over the Bear River, which even now is the most substantial bridge in Petoskey. As he walks, Yogi thinks about the fact that he does not desire the librarian at the Petoskey Public Library (where Hemingway gave his post-World War I speech) and that he is not interested in any of a group of high school girls on their way home.

> *Yogi walked on up the hill and turned to the left onto the Charlevoix road. He passed the last houses of the outskirts of Petoskey and came out onto the open country road. On his right was a field that stretched to Little Traverse Bay. The blue of the bay opening out into the big Lake Michigan. Across the bay the pine hills behind Harbor Springs.* [Hemingway spelled "Harbor" correctly here.] *Beyond, where you could not see it, Cross Village, where the Indians lived. Even further beyond, the Straits of Mackinac with St. Ignace . . .*[5]

The field stretching to Little Traverse Bay still affords a view of the bay opening into Lake Michigan with the pine hills behind Harbor Springs, now laced with the ski trails of two of the Midwest's highest ski areas.

As Yogi sits watching the sunset, two Indians stop and talk to him. They ask him for a "chew of tobacco" and liquor, and he gives them a "package of Peerless" (Billy Tabeshaw's favorite in "Sepi Jingan") and his pocket flask. One Indian points to the sky as the home of "gitchy Manitou the Mighty" (here Hemingway uses again the Indian word, "Manitou"). They said that they had both been at "Carlisle Indian School." When interviewed, Mrs. Joseph Otis said an Indian school by that name did exist.

Yogi returned to Petoskey with the Indians when the sunset faded. The three of them went past the feed store, crossed the bridge over the Bear River, and "climbed the hill that led past Doctor Rumsey's house and the Home Tea-Room to the pool-room."[6] Doctor Rumsey's name is similar to Doctor Ramsdell's, but no one in Petoskey remembered a "Home Tea-Room" located on Main Street.

Yogi Johnson then resolves his lack of desire for the librarian and the high school girls by following a naked squaw who is thrown out of the beanery while he is there. They follow the G.R. & I. railroad tracks "stretching North toward Mackinaw City and St. Ignace."[7] Yogi starts on the first lap of the trip Nick Adams took in "Big Two-Hearted River." Yogi is soon clad only in his pump-maker shoes, as he walks naked beside the unclad squaw who is carrying her papoose on her back. Her husky dog whines and licks Yogi's ankles—a friendly Indian dog again by the railroad tracks which is disquietingly reminiscent of "Sepi Jingan."

At the end of Part III Hemingway, in a Fieldingesque note to the reader, makes a statement.

> *Anyway, H. G. Wells asked us if perhaps our reader would not think too much of this story is autobiographical. Please, reader, just get that idea out of your head. We have lived in Petoskey, Michigan, it is true, and naturally many of the characters are drawn from life as we lived it then. But they are other people, not the author.*[8]

What Hemingway wrote in the note to the reader was certainly true of *The Torrents of Spring*. This novel is not autobiographical, although Hemingway again uses real names and describes actual places. But the young writer made his characters do things he had experienced himself, which shows that his Petoskey days had been absorbed and turned into fiction. From the activities of the characters in *Torrents*, it is not difficult to reconstruct the activities of the twenty-year-old writer living in the northern town.

Today anyone can recreate a day Hemingway could have spent in Petoskey and follow the exact footsteps that the author or his fictional characters took around the town on a typical day. He might have left Potter's house on

State Street after breakfast and walked down the hill to the Public Library, where he could have read many of the newspapers and magazines listed in *Torrents*. Then he could have walked over to the railroad station to check on train schedules for forthcoming fishing trips. From the station Hemingway could have walked up the street leading away from the lake and to the barber shop, possibly for a shave, and anyone who wants to take a walk around Petoskey even now can do the same. Hemingway might have had lunch at a "beanery" and then walked down Main Street. Later he could have stood on the Bear River bridge and watched the water rush towards the lake as anyone with a few minutes to spare can do today.

Hemingway, walking with a limp, would probably soon have left the bridge and hurried back along Main Street, then turned up the hill toward the high school. He must have watched the high school girls, as Yogi Johnson did, as he waited for Marjorie Bump. If she were late, he might have gone into the Catholic church across the street from Petoskey High School and lit a candle, as he describes in one of his letters to Grace Quinlan.

In the evening Hemingway, as his characters in *Torrents* did, might have gone by himself down to the Petoskey harbor or sat on a log in the lonely field outside of town and watched the sunset over Little Traverse Bay.

Twenty-first Birthday

After he left Petoskey, Hemingway had a successful winter and early spring in Toronto writing free-lance articles for the Toronto *Star Weekly*. After his discouraging autumn in Petoskey when he had all of his work rejected, Hemingway regained his self-confidence with the writing of articles which were published under his own byline and for which he was paid. He sold fifteen articles and was paid less than one hundred and fifty dollars for them, but he was doing what he wanted to do: writing.

In the late spring of 1920 Hemingway left Toronto for northern Michigan to fish for trout. Soon the spring turned into summer, his coming-of-age summer when Hemingway had a quarrel with his mother which severed his ties to his parents (Doctor Hemingway also became involved in the disagreement) and freed him to write candidly about them without remorse or guilt.

The summer started in an ordinary way, but slowly the Hemingway family conflicts grew to dramatic proportions. Ernest was staying at Horton Bay when Mrs. Hemingway and the other children arrived at Walloon Lake on the first of June. Doctor Hemingway was practicing medicine and sweltering through a hot, humid summer in Illinois. When the children had been young, the doctor had spent most of each summer at Walloon, but when they were grown, he spent only two weeks there. Mrs. Hemingway expected her oldest son to come to help her open the cottage and do all of the needed work. In other words, she expected Ernest to fill the role of his father. He rebelled, probably for two reasons. The first reason was that his mother did not accept his writing (free-lance though it was) as an occupation and derided him for being unemployed, and the second reason was that it was probable he consciously or unconsciously did not want to take over his father's role.

In his writing, Hemingway has put a definite accent on manliness. At times he almost seems to make a cult of manliness, but this emphasis does not have the easy explanation which certain critics would like it to have. Hemingway recognized that his mother had taken advantage of his father, who was a gentleman and believed in the Christian virtues. Ernest did not want to let her get her way with him also. She had always been able to shirk responsibility with her well-timed headaches at times of crisis and with her inability to deal with any routine feminine duties, such as housework, cooking, or even taking care of her own children.

Ernest rebelled at fifteen and turned to the lonely sports of fishing and hunting. Not content with his mother's Victorianism and escapism, he decided to find out about some of the hard truths of the outside world. Strongheaded, independent in action, and certain of his basic convictions, Hemingway confronted his mother, who might have made a sissy of a less strong son. During the summer of his twenty-first birthday, he became strong and vehement. He knew that he must be extra strong to be free, to be able to be a writer, and not to fall into the trap which had ensnared his long-suffering father.

As soon as she arrived at Walloon Lake, Mrs. Hemingway began her complaints about Ernest in her letters to

Doctor Hemingway. A record of the correspondence that summer between Doctor and Mrs. Hemingway is included in Leicester Hemingway's book. What was missing, though, were letters from Ernest telling what he thought of the situation. Fortunately, Ernest wrote Grace Quinlan about his eventful twenty-first summer, and now his side of the story is also available. Although his letters cannot be quoted directly, their meaning and content can be given to present his point of view at the time of the action.

The first letters which Doctor Hemingway wrote to his wife that summer, were in response to her complaints. In the first one, written on June eleventh, the doctor expressed hope that Ernest had been over to help her. On June thirteenth, Doctor Hemingway promised to write Ernest and again hoped he had "been over and helped . . ." On June sixteenth he wrote his wife to let her know that Ernest had written him to say that he expected to go over to see her soon and had been working hard with Bill. Bill must again be Bill Smith, but whether their work was at the Charleses or not Doctor Hemingway does not explain in his letter. On June nineteenth he was "pleased to know Ernest has been over to see you."[1]

Until July second, when Doctor Hemingway went to Walloon Lake for his two-week vacation, his only mention of his eldest son in his letters was a plan for Ernest to kill the rabbits in the garden at Walloon with his .22. He also reported the fact that he had received a postcard from Ted Brumback, who wrote from Vanderbilt, Michigan, of a fishing trip on the Black River with Ernest. Ted Brumback was the son of a prominent Kansas City family and had met Hemingway when they both worked on the Kansas City *Star*. Brumback joined the ambulance corps of the Italian Army at the same time Hemingway did, was on the same fishing trip when they received their overseas

orders, and shared a tent with Hemingway in Italy during
the First World War.

After his short vacation, Doctor Hemingway returned
to Oak Park and wrote a letter to Mrs. Hemingway dated
July eighteenth:

> *I have written Ernest and sent the check as we talked
> over. I advised him to go with Ted down Travers* [sic] *City way and work at good wages and at least cut down
> his living expenses. I also most sincerely hoped now
> that he had attained the legal age he would be more con-
> siderate of others and use less vitriolistic* [sic] *words.*[2]

On July twenty-first the doctor wrote:

> *. . . Today is Ernest's twenty-first birthday anniver-
> sary and I hope he will have a good day. He has not
> written me yet, but I took for granted he had done the
> spraying as per your Thursday letter, and so sent him
> the five dollars and birthday five. I hope he will now
> write me a good letter . . .*[3]

On July twenty-second, the day after the birthday
incident, Doctor Hemingway wrote to his wife:

> *I think Ernest is trying to irritate us in some way, so
> as to have a witness in Brummy* [Ted Brumback] *in
> hearing us say we would be glad if he was to go away
> and stay.* [Possibly the doctor and his wife told Ernest
> this when the doctor was at Walloon on vacation and
> Ted Brumback had been there to hear it.] *I have written
> him that I wanted him to get busy and be more self-sup-
> porting and respectful, and leave the Bay and go to
> work down Travers* [sic] *City way. I will write to him
> and enclose herewith for you to read and hand to him.
> Keep up your courage, my darling. We are all at work
> and very soon he will settle down and suffer the loss of
> his friends the way he is fast using them up. He will*

*have to move into new fields to conquer . . . You
read Ernest's letter enclosed! If he is gone, seal it, and
stamp it and mail it to him!*[4]

The differences between Ernest and his father are
clearly shown in Doctor Hemingway's letters. The doctor
became self-righteous and unable to understand his son or
his motivations. Ernest was certainly not "using up" his
friends—in fact, they sustained him through his estrangement from his family.

On July twenty-fifth Doctor Hemingway wrote an
answer to a letter from Mrs. Hemingway about Ernest's
twenty-first-birthday dinner:

> *In the last mail last night I received your big en-
> velope letter and the letter of Thursday evening, after
> Ernest's birthday supper. I hope he went back to the
> Bay with Bill and that you read and have mailed him
> the letter I wrote to him to stay away from Windemere
> until he was again invited. You surely gave him and his
> friends a good time . . .*[5]

From the doctor's reply Mrs. Hemingway must have
described only the nicer aspects of the birthday dinner
evening and omitted most of what had really happened.

In a letter which Ernest Hemingway wrote on August
ninth and mailed to Grace Quinlan from Boyne City,
Michigan, he described what had happened on July 21,
1920. He referred to it as "the kicking out business." According to Ernest, he was invited by his sisters, Ursula and
Sunny, and two other girls, who arranged a "midnight supper" which included Ernest and Ted Brumback, neither of
whom was interested in going. The whole group (Ursula, Sunny, Bob Loomis and his sister with their houseguest, plus Jean Reynolds, Ted Brumback, and Ernest)
went to a place called Ryan's Point to eat and returned to
the Hemingway cottage at three A.M.

According to Ernest, Mrs. Loomis realized that her son and daughter and their houseguest were missing and frantically ran to the Hemingway cottage. She accused Ernest and Brumback of organizing the party for some foul purpose, although the truth was the two older boys had been persuaded to go and acted more as chaperones.

Mrs. Hemingway permanently "kicked out" Ernest and his friend the next morning without letting them tell their side of the story. Ernest felt that she was glad to have an excuse to banish him, because he felt that she more or less hated him, since he had opposed her decision to spend two or three thousand dollars to build a new cottage for herself ("Grace Cottage" at "Longfield," across the lake from "Windemere") instead of sending her younger children to college.

Doctor Hemingway wrote a letter to his wife on July twenty-sixth which shows that he did not receive the full story from her and had made up his mind against Ernest.

My dear Gracie: I have just received your letter written Saturday the 24th and am indeed sorry for you. I hope you have handed Ernest the letter that I am enclosing for him, advising him he must move on and get to work and stay away from Windemere until he is invited to return. It is a great insult that he and Ted Brumback should take it for granted that they can lay down on the family as they have been doing. I supposed of course they would have gone back to the Bay when Bill Smith went back the night after the wonderful 21st supper you wrote about. . . . I so wish that Ernest would show some decent loyalty to you and not keep on the sponge game with his friend Ted. I will write to him again at the Bay, so if he is still at Windemere tell him that you know there is mail for him at the Bay. I will also write Ted at the Bay advising him that it is altogether too much for you to entertain him longer at Windemere, and request that he and Ernest not return to Windemere until they are invited by you. . . . It is hard to work here in the heat, but harder to know that you are suffering such insults as to cause the breaking up of the family circle. . . . I shall continue to pray for Ernest, that he will develop a sense of greater responsibility, for if he does not the Great Creator will cause him to suffer a whole lot more than he ever has so far.[8]

On July twenty-eighth Doctor Hemingway wrote a long letter about Ernest to his wife:

My darlings at Windemere: I have received a very definite letter of denial from Ernest. He is a very unusual youth that does not realize that his mother and father have done a lot more for him than any of his chums. He is sure to suffer a lot. I will pay no attention to his statements that he has done nothing wrong at Windemere. He says Brummy was there at your particular request and that he had painted the house for you and dug garbage holes and washed dishes and done all the work of a "hired hand." Let it go. If they will only now stay away from irritating you. He says in a letter to Father [Grandfather Hemingway] that he lost his pocketbook while fishing on Spring Brook and in it was the cash of a check from Father for the two dollars. He did not tell me a kind thing. All denial of my statements as to the reasons I was sure it was best for he and Brummy to stay away from Windemere until he was again invited by you. He says he does not want to hear from me any more along those lines. I hope it will not be necessary. He does not answer a question about their trip that I spoke of to him. I shall not let his fiery letter bother me and I will wait a while to write him again. Reading over the copies I am sure I only wrote just what you would want me to do. In his letter to Father he was as sweet as pie. Said he saw all his Connable friends from Toronto in Petoskey last Sunday.[7]

Ernest had obviously defended his point of view in his letter to his father. Unfortunately, Doctor Hemingway was so emotional about the language Ernest used and the fact that he preferred the company of his friends to his parents that the doctor was unable to be objective about the situation. He took his wife's side without looking at Ernest's side. In his letter the doctor also reveals the generosity of Grandfather Hemingway and the respect Ernest held for him.

On July thirtieth Doctor Hemingway wrote his strongest anti-Ernest letter:

I am greatly relieved to know Ernest has at last gone, and trust he will stay away and now you can get what you so much need this summer. [What did Mrs. Hemingway need? Rest?] *The last act of his was his finish, and it will be just so all along the line.* [Was the "last act" the letter he wrote to the doctor?] *Oh, if he alone could do the suffering. I am glad that Ursula is having a few days at Marjorie Bumps. Hope she will not see Ernest. . . . If those big boys had gumption at all they would have volunteered all the paint work and had it done long ago . . . I am anxious for you to tell me what Ted had to say when you delivered your ultimatum. Ernest's last letter to me after reading the one I sent you to hand him, does not require an answer. It was written in anger and was filled with expressions that were untrue to a gentleman and a son who has had everything done for him. We have done too much. He must get busy and make his own way, and suffering alone will be the means of softening his Iron Heart of selfishness. . . .*[8]

After he left "Windemere," Ernest went first to Horton Bay and then on a fishing trip to the Black River. In a letter he wrote to Grace Quinlan from Horton Bay on August first he said he felt unjustly accused by his parents and was a bit blue. Ernest was upset about being fired from his home, kicked out quite permanently, and not having any home even if he did not plan to use it. Hemingway mentioned that Ursula was in Petoskey visiting Red (probably Marj Bump, for she had red hair) and that Grace might have heard the whole story from her. He wanted to write a long letter to Grace but did not, because he felt low and lonesome in spite of eight boarders being right in the same room (probably at the Dilworths').

On August eighth Ernest wrote a long letter filled with excellent descriptions. He had a marvelous time on the trip with Ted Brumback, Jacques Pentecost, someone nicknamed "the Fever," and Dick Smoke, who was an Indian friend of Ernest's. They slept around a campfire under a full moon, and Brumback played the mandolin and afterward Ernest read Lord Dunsany's murder tales out loud. Bill Smith and Doctor and Mrs. Charles came out to the river, and they all caught fifty trout for the couple to take home.

Hemingway wrote in the same letter about his twenty-first-birthday dinner and mentioned that he received three or four letters from his family but had not opened them. He felt so disgusted with his family that he did not care to have anything more to do with them at least for a year.

He then listed all of the things he wanted to do that winter: drive around the United States with Jacques Pentecost, return to Italy, work on a newspaper, or get a job in New York. Hemingway was drawn between two main plans; he could not decide whether to get another writing job (which he did do in Chicago) or to travel. When he thought of boarding a tramp steamer, he became poetic in his descriptions of the ocean, the boat, and the sensations of a sea voyage. Hemingway ended his list of desires when he wrote Miss Quinlan that he wanted to lie chin down on a grassy cliff overlooking the sea.

His father was more mellow in his letter of August twenty-seventh:

> *. . . I had a nice letter from Ernest today, written yesterday in Petoskey. He says he has been fishing with Sam Nickey* [Ernest also mentioned fishing with him in his August first letter to Miss Quinlan.] *and had some good times, and had some wonderful fishing. He surely feels as if he had a great injustice done him at Windemere. I do not in any way discuss the matter with him. I am glad he has cooled off and again writes to his father, who will always love him, and will continue to pray for him to be an honest and unselfish and considerate Christian gentleman and loyal to those who love him.*[9]

Ernest's father had forgiven him a month after the incident, but Mrs. Hemingway wrote another letter to Ernest chastising him and sent a copy to her husband. Doctor Hemingway began to wonder whether everything his wife had told him about the birthday incident was as she had presented it; on September fifteenth he wrote:

> *I continue to pray for Ernest and believe that God will soften his heart and that we all shall again be united in love. If you falsely accused him, be sure to beg his pardon, even if he had made many mistakes. For false accusations grow more sore all the time and separate many dear friends and relatives . . .*[10]

On September nineteenth the doctor gave his wife some good advice in a letter: "Love him my dear, he is our boy and we must always love and forgive each other . . ."[11]

What actually happened on Ernest's birthday to cause the rift between himself and his parents is still a little unclear. From the Doctor's and Ernest's letters the events can be partially reconstructed. Apparently, tension had existed between Ernest and his mother before the birthday dinner, and at the dinner she handed him a letter commanding him to leave "Windemere" and not to return until he was invited back. She must have misrepresented to her husband what she had done, and he, unwittingly, wrote Ernest a letter telling him what Mrs. Hemingway wanted told. At the end of the summer Doctor Hemingway had forgiven his son, but the damage was done.

That fall Ernest returned to Chicago but not to his home; instead he moved in with some of his Horton Bay friends, who had been kind to him. Ernest never forgot what his mother had done to him and to his friend, Ted Brumback, who was supposedly invited to "Windemere" by Mrs. Hemingway as a houseguest. Although Ernest helped his mother financially when she became a widow and was more forgiving and generous to her than she was to him, he never spared her in his fictional accounts about his parents.

Michigan Wedding

Ernest Hemingway and the woman he wanted to marry, Hadley Richardson, decided to come to northern Michigan for their marriage and honeymoon. Charlevoix County was the scene of their wedding—the ceremony was performed in the little town of Horton Bay—and the records of their marriage remain in the Charlevoix courthouse. After the wedding the young couple spent their honeymoon at the Hemingway cottage on Walloon Lake. Again Hemingway had returned to Michigan.

The town of Charlevoix, located on a channel between Lake Michigan and Lake Charlevoix, was named for Father Pierre François Xavier de Charlevoix, who was born in 1682 during the reign of Louis XIV. Father Charlevoix, a Jesuit, attracted the attention of the Regent of France, through his historical writings, and was sent on a mission to America. On June 18, 1721, Father Charlevoix left Fort Ponchartrain at Detroit to make the canoe trip to Michilimackinac. With two large canoes, eight attendants, and a companion, he reached Mackinaw in ten days. He traveled down Lake Michigan, stopped at Beaver Island, and paddled past the site of the future town of Charlevoix. Father Charlevoix and his companions survived the long canoe trip down Lake Michigan and through the Mississippi to return to France, where he wrote his *Histoire de la nouvelle France.*

What is now Charlevoix County was wilderness until 1846, when a colony of Mormons under James Jesse Strang settled on Beaver Island. Soon after—in 1852—the town of Charlevoix was established by non-Mormon fishermen. On July 13, 1854, a skirmish between the mainland fishermen and the island-dwelling Mormons resulted in a Mormon victory, and the small settlement of outnumbered fishermen was frightened away. The town was abandoned until later in the same year, when two Mormon families arrived at Pine River (the early name of Charlevoix) to find everything just as the former occupants had left it. The Mormon settlers were soon joined by other pioneers, non-Mormons, who left after years of being attacked by their Mormon neighbors.

James Strang appointed himself king over the colony he established on Beaver Island. King Strang ruled his Mormon kingdom with his many wives and tamed his subjects at a whipping post, until 1856, when he was assassinated by Thomas Bedford, a Mormon subject who had had a falling out with the "king."

The Mormons were driven from Beaver Island and Charlevoix after Strang's assassination, and many of the former, non-Mormon settlers returned to the territory to recover their land. The town of Charlevoix grew; the river was dredged; a bridge was built, making the little ferry obsolete.

With the dredging of the river, in 1883, Charlevoix became one of the major ports in the area for loading timber on sailing schooners. The lumber camp on Walloon Lake near the Hemingway cottage (mentioned in the story "Indian Camp") and the mill at Horton Bay on Lake Charlevoix (mentioned in "The End of Something" and "Up in Michigan") both hauled their timber to Charlevoix to be shipped to all points on the Great Lakes.

Charlevoix retains little of the appearance of the rough lumbering port, for now it is a neat resort town of frame houses, clapboard inns, and summer cottages. The water in the channel between Lake Michigan and Lake Charlevoix passes the year-round homes on its banks and flows under the bridge at the center of town. During the summer months the Charlevoix harbor has many large yachts moored at the public docks. In the private boat clubs and boatyards flanking the banks of the channel other large sailboats and cabin cruisers constantly are being refurbished, refueled, or just being held at moorage. At the narrow entrance to Lake Charlevoix, where the railroad bridge spans the inlet, two summer resorts face each other from opposite banks. On the north is the Chicago Club and its surrounding cluster of large summer homes, and on the southern bank is the Belvedere Association (established in 1878) with gaily-colored cabanas on its white-sand beach.

During the summer of 1920, Hemingway often played tennis with Ted Brumback, Bill Smith, and Dr. Charles in Charlevoix. On August ninth of that summer in a letter to Edith Quinlan, he described his experience at a gambling place named Cooks, in the town of Charlevoix. He had just been "kicked out" of his family's summer cottage and was thinking about finding work at the cement plant in Petoskey, until the night he played roulette until two in the morning. Hemingway started with six dollars and had won fifty-nine when the group he was with wanted to go home. He wrote that he quit with his profit and was saved from the cement plant.

In the early fall of 1920 Hemingway returned to Chicago to work for the *Co-operative Commonwealth*. He lived first with Bill Horne in an attic bedroom until Y. K. Smith, the eldest of the Smith family, offered to let Hemingway and Horne share a bedroom in his large apartment on East Chicago Avenue, and there Hemingway met Hadley Richardson, a friend of Y. K.'s sister, Kate Smith.

Hemingway was employed as an associate editor of the

Co-operative Commonwealth, a monthly house organ run by Frank Parker Stockbridge, a Chicago advertising man, from autumn, 1920, until December, 1921. The house organ turned out to be an illegal venture encouraging subscribers to invest in a corporation which eventually went bankrupt in 1922.

In August, 1921, Hemingway wrote two letters to Miss Grace Quinlan about marriage, Hadley, and his job with the *Co-operative Commonwealth*. The first letter was mailed from Goshen, Indiana, on August seventh. The young writer was driving a car from the East to Chicago for his boss, probably Mr. Stockbridge. Miss Quinlan had written to him suggesting he was too young to be married, and Hemingway explained in a letter to Miss Quinlan that he and Hadley had felt exactly the same way until they realized life would be as interesting as the pseudo-Gothic hotel pictured on the stationery unless they could have each other to live with. He felt that in circumstances such as theirs a person had to make allowances. He then wrote that he had never wanted to be married before, even though he had faced it on numerous occasions. He enclosed in the letter a photograph of Hadley in her wedding dress, which he noted was very improper to show to anyone before the wedding, but that he wanted to let Grace see it anyhow.

In a letter written on the *Co-operative Commonwealth* stationery and mailed from Chicago on August nineteenth, Hemingway expressed interest in the rumors circulating about him concerning a previous marriage. He wanted to know whether people had him married in France, whether he deserted his supposed bride, and he asked Grace whether she thought he would be a bigamist when he married Hadley. (He had not been married before; these were just rumors.)

Immediately following his paragraph about the marriage rumors, he enthusiastically wrote about his pre-wedding plans. He was to leave Chicago on the twenty-seventh of August, arrive at Walloon the next day, and immediately leave for the Sturgeon River for the last three days of the fishing season. When he mentioned fishing, he wrote that it had been so long that he was starved and crazy for it. On September first the future bridegroom planned to return to Horton Bay to prepare for the wedding. He felt that it would be a fairly high grade occasion and a good gang would be there. He thought that not many people would be at Horton Bay for the wedding, but many of the people he liked would.

At the time Hemingway wrote the letter, he noted that "Hash" (Hadley's nickname) was in the Upper Peninsula of Michigan having all of the fun for both of them and that he would not see her again until Horton Bay. He noted that his parents were at Walloon; his sister, "Sunny," in Minnesota, and one of his other sisters, "Marce," in Maine. All of the people he knew in Chicago had left town, and the large city was as "lonely as Boyne Falls."

In the same letter he commented about how civilized he had become. He dated the beginning of his civilization as being about twelve months previous. Although he did not relate the two facts in his letter, it is interesting to note that he had also known Hadley for almost twelve months.

The young writer wrote this letter during his lunch hour; after lunch he had to interview the president of the U. S. Grain Growers, Inc. The house organ had to go to press in three days, and Hemingway had been working overtime in order to have material prepared to cover the time he would take for his wedding and honeymoon. At that time he was writing a hundred-thousand-word book for the *Co-operative Commonwealth* which was being published in five-thousand-word installments. He felt the book was deadly stuff and classified himself as a wreck.

The record of Hemingway's first wedding has been moved to the new County Courthouse in Charlevoix. In the record book he used his middle initial, M., for Miller, when he gave his name. He apparently used the middle initial only in his articles for the Toronto *Star Weekly* and for legal documents. Years later, one of the few written instructions he had placed in a safety deposit box before his death was signed "Ernest M. Hemingway."

In the courthouse in the small resort town, the Hemingway entry in the ledger book appears as fresh as if it were written a year ago, instead of in 1921. The wedding is listed on a page beside many others, with the information that he was married on September 3, 1921, by the Reverend W. J. Dateon, who was rector of Emmanuel Church. Thus was solved a problem which existed for the prospective bridegroom several weeks before the wedding.

On August 19, 1921, he had written a humorous letter to Miss Quinlan asking for her help in selecting a minister. In his letter, in what is almost an aside, Hemingway wants to know if she can recommend a capable minister, preacher, priest, or prelate to perform the ceremony. The engaged couple preferred either a Presbyterian or an Episcopalian, although Hemingway wrote that it did not make any difference to him. He wrote that he and Hadley had thought of Bishop Tuttle from St. Louis, who summered at Harbor Point, but added that the Bishop would probably have returned to St. Louis by September.

Although the young writer suggested a Presbyterian or an Episcopalian and was married in the Methodist Church at Horton Bay by the rector of Emmanuel Church, he used the Catholic word "priest" when referring to a minister. Hemingway was probably more of a Catholic than a member of any other religion, even as early as 1921. His grandfather, Anson Tyler Hemingway, was a Congregationalist, his Grandfather Hall was an Episcopalian, and his parents were Congregationalists, but their son had become attracted to the Catholic Church when he was in Italy. He was later officially converted to the Catholic faith when he married Pauline Pfeiffer, who was a Roman Catholic.

In a letter written to Grace Quinlan on September 30, 1920, Hemingway mentioned that he had gone to the Catholic church with Kate Smith, Bill Smith's sister. He wrote that he had burned a candle and had prayed for all the things he wanted but thought he would never be able to get. He added that he was in a very fine mood when he came out of the church, and in a short time the Lord had sent an "Adventure with a touch of Romance" to reward him. He classified it as a very small adventure, which was unexpected and for the moment thrilling. It is evident that he connected the adventure with going to the church, because he added in his letter he was glad that he had burned the candle. Unfortunately, Hemingway did not describe the romantic adventure in his letter, but instead told Grace Quinlan to ask another girl for the details. In his postscript he mentioned that he had burned a candle for Grace, who received the letter, and he wondered if it had had any results, because he had prayed she would receive anything she wanted. His Catholicism, which is reflected in this letter of September 30, 1920, seems to resemble an Italian more than an American attitude toward Catholicism.

Hemingway's funeral in 1961 was conducted by the Reverend Robert J. Waldman, pastor of Our Lady of the Snows Catholic Church in Sun Valley, Idaho. He told a reporter, "Mr. Hemingway was entitled to burial rites of the Roman Catholic Church, although he was not as good a member as some others."[1] Before the funeral Hemingway's older son, John, was asked if his father was a Catholic at the time of his death, and he answered: "He actually wasn't. No." Father Waldman countered Hemingway's son's reply by stating to the Associated Press that as far as he knew, Hemingway officially had not left or rejected the Church. He said that the simple rites which he conducted were "due to the family's request, which we are following."

Father Waldman also added that the church accepted the ruling of the authorities that Hemingway had died of a self-inflicted gunshot wound in the head. The officials in Ketchum, Idaho, where Hemingway died, had made no determination of whether the shooting was accidental or otherwise. The priest stated that the church would "not go beyond the ruling of the authorities."

In August of 1921, before Hemingway was married for the first time or had met Pauline Pfeiffer or had lived in Ketchum, Idaho, his requirements for the priest who was to marry him took a humorous turn when he outlined them in the previously mentioned letter. Hadley did not care what kind of priest it was (according to Hemingway), but he wrote that she preferred a breed of priest who did not wear a celluloid collar or chew tobacco. Hemingway then insisted that the priest must have the ability to read and be dignified. In a mock-serious tone the future bridegroom wrote that it was dignity they were paying the prelate for, and they did not want an evangelist, who would shout "Praise be the Lord" and roll around the floor at a critical moment during the ceremony.

The Charlevoix courthouse record lists the bridegroom's witnesses as William B. Smith and George J. Breaker, both of St. Louis. Bill Smith was Hemingway's good friend at Horton Bay, after whom he modeled a character in "The End of Something" and "The Three-Day Blow." George Breaker was the man who gave the bride away. Mr. Breaker's wife, Helen, was Hadley's matron of honor. Since her own father was not alive, Hadley asked George Breaker to give her away. Mr. Breaker was a lawyer and several years older than the bride. The future bridegroom gave his age as twenty-three, although he was really only twenty-two at the time. Hadley Richardson, his future bride, gave the officials her true age, thirty.

Hemingway listed his occupation as "journalist," and Hadley described her occupation as "housework," which was an indication of her unpretentious character. She played the piano well and could have classified herself as a musician, but instead she already thought of herself as a housewife. Hadley was not to become an ordinary house-wife though; she was the home-oriented woman who was glorified in *A Moveable Feast*, a homemaker who was married to two of the most important literary and newspaper figures of the twentieth century. Since 1933 she has been married to Paul Scott Mowrer, who was Chief of the European Wire Service of the Chicago *Daily News*, had been editor of the *News* for eleven years, and is the author of thirteen books.

When Hemingway married Hadley at Horton Bay, he invited everyone in the surrounding area who was his friend; therefore the Hemingway-Richardson wedding was probably the largest one ever held in the little town on Lake Charlevoix. Everyone who attended remembers it vividly, but as is the usual case with eyewitnesses, the testimony differs from one witness to the next.

One of the most interesting versions of the wedding is recounted by a good friend of Hemingway's who was a contemporary and drinking companion. "At the wedding everyone was waiting in the church for the ceremony to begin, but the bride couldn't be found anywhere. Finally somebody went to look for her and found her swimming down in the lake. They told her she was late, so she hurried up and put on her white wedding dress. 'Hash,' that's what Ernie called her, because she was his meal ticket, had sopping wet hair throughout the whole wedding." (Mrs. Mowrer denied this story.) Describing who came to the wedding and what happened at the reception, the same friend continued, "Doc and Mrs. Hemingway brought all their children to the wedding in a horse-drawn carriage. The people from the Italian Consulate in Detroit or somewhere down in the south part of the state came to the wedding and brought along a lot of wine. Everyone got roaring drunk, and we all ended up at the Dilworths'."

Another picture of the wedding was painted by Mrs. Wesley Dilworth of Boyne City, Michigan, who, although she was a young girl at the time of the ceremony, remembers "my mother-in-law, Mrs. James Dilworth, serving a wedding breakfast in her cottage when they were married." Mrs. Wesley Dilworth, now a grey-haired woman with mild manners, gave her version of the Hemingways' participation in the wedding preparations: "Even though Ernest's parents attended the wedding, most of the preparations and details about the reception were handled by Mrs. Charles and my mother-in-law. The wedding breakfast was cooked in 'Pinehurst,' a Dilworth cottage, and served in 'Shangri-la,' another house belonging to the Dilworth family."

Another resident of Horton Bay at the time, Stanley Van Hoesen, gave his account of the wedding which he had attended when he was ten years old: "It was held in the Methodist Church which burned down. It was a frame church, painted white, like the general store. Ernie and my father, George Van Hoesen, had been out fishing on the Black River, and Ernie was late to his own wedding. They had gone over to the Black in a horse and buggy. Ernie was all dirty and had to wash up before the ceremony. Everyone in Horton Bay was invited to the wedding, and it was a big affair. It was a nice day, and they were married about two in the afternoon. Hadley was a redhead, as I remember."

Several other people who attended the ceremony were not clear as to whether it was Ernest or Hadley who was late to the wedding or whether anyone was late at all. They all agreed, though, that the two were married in the white, frame Methodist Church in Horton Bay and that September 3, 1921, was a beautiful, clear day.

Both Ernest Hemingway's sister Marcelline and his brother Leicester wrote about the wedding and their sister-in-law in their respective biographies of their famous brother. Marcelline Hemingway Sanford, who was a year older than her brother Ernest, describes the Horton Bay wedding, as follows:

> Ernest told us that he and Hadley were going to be married. We liked her so much, we were all tremendously pleased. Mother and Dad offered them Windemere Cottage when Ernest and Hadley told us of their plans for a summer wedding up north.
>
> On the third of September, 1921, they were married in the little white Methodist Church next to the general store in Horton Bay. The informal reception for the families and the few close friends was held at Aunty Beth Dilworth's home across the road from the church.
>
> Ernest and Bill Smith, Carl Edgar, Bill Horne, and the other friends who served as ushers wore blue coats and white flannel trousers. Hadley, of course, was dressed in white and wore a veil. Her parents were not living, but her brother-in-law and sister, Professor and Mrs. Roland G. Usher of Washington University, came on from St. Louis; the Connables, summering in Petoskey, were present; and of course, the Hemingway family.
>
> The young couple spent their honeymoon that balmy September in our family cottage, Windemere, which our parents and younger children had vacated just before the wedding day.[2]

Although Leicester Hemingway was only six at the time of the wedding, he remembers it in more detail than the late Mrs. Sanford. He recalls Hadley as being "a tall, well-formed, English-looking girl," and states that the reason the couple chose to be married in Michigan was that "Ernest was strong for Horton's Bay and Hadley liked the idea of spending some time in northern Michigan after the wedding."³ Leicester describes the town of Horton Bay on September 3, 1921, with the elm trees along the highway covered with dust. He recalls that the wedding party gathered beyond the general store and walked down to the Methodist Church for the four o'clock wedding. During the ceremony the younger brother was impressed by the flowers, the organist from the Episcopal Church in Petoskey playing the wedding march, the angelic-looking bride, but the one event which shocked him was the bridegroom walking down the aisle to be married, with shaking legs.

The official announcement about the wedding, which Doctor Hemingway wrote for the newspapers, appeared as follows:

> *Ernest Miller Hemingway, First Lieutenant in the Italian Army during the World War and son of Dr. and Mrs. Clarence E. Hemingway of Oak Park, was married at Horton's Bay, Michigan, on September 3, 1921, to Miss Hadley Richardson of St. Louis, Missouri. The young couple preferred a simple country wedding and honeymoon spent at Windemere, Walloon Lake, Michigan, the summer home of the Hemingways, to the usual formal church wedding in St. Louis. The little white church at Horton's Bay was decorated with masses of swamp lilies, bittersweet, and boughs of balsam. After the ceremony a dinner was served at Pinehurst Cottage to the bridal party, consisting of Miss Catherine Foster Smith of Chicago, Miss Ruth Bradfield and Mrs. D. Charles of St. Louis, and Mrs. Roland C. Usher, sister of the bride, and Mrs. George J. Breaker of St. Louis, Mr. William D. Smith, Mr. George J. Breaker, Mr. J. C. Edgar of St. Joseph, Missouri, Mr. William D. Horne, Jr. of Yonkers, N.Y., Howell Griffiths Jenkins of Chicago, and Arther Meyer. The last three were in the*

Italian service with the groom. Mr. George J. Breaker
gave the bride away in the absence of Professor Usher.
Other guests at the dinner were Mrs. Ralph Connable
and son of Toronto, Mr. Edwin Pailthorpe and Mr.
Luman Ramsdell of Petoskey, Michigan, Dr. and Mrs.
Clarence E. Hemingway, Misses Ursula and Carol
Hemingway and Master Leicester Hemingway, of Oak
Park. Many telegrams were received from people of
high social and state positions in Italy where Lieutenant
Hemingway received such signal honors and decora-
tions at the close of the war. The young couple expect
to spend the winter in Italy.[4]

Even the Hemingway family did not agree about who
came to the wedding and what happened. Marcelline has
Mr. Usher attending the wedding, while Doctor Hemingway wrote that he was absent. (Mrs. Mowrer could not
remember if Roland Usher came to the wedding, but she
thought he did not come with her sister, Mrs. Usher.)
Neither Doctor Hemingway nor Marcelline noted the
attendance of the Italians. Doctor Hemingway, in his
desire to make his own family and Ernest seem important,
did not mention anything in his announcement about Hadley's education. Marcelline writes about "Aunty Beth Dilworth," as if the Hemingways had planned the entire
reception, while Mrs. Wesley Dilworth remembers it
differently. Ursula Hemingway Jepson recently wrote in
a letter: "Marcelline couldn't give an accurate description
of Ernie's wedding to Hadley, because she wasn't there.
Carol, Leicester, and I were the only brother and sisters
there. I remember Hadley as being perfectly beautiful and
composed."

After Hemingway's death, the *New York Post* ran a
feature serial, "The Hemingway Story," by Alfred G.
Aronowitz and Pete Hamill. As an example of the different versions of facts concerning Hadley, the wedding, and
the honeymoon, the paragraph referring to it follows:

His first wife was Hadley Richardson, a beautiful, red-haired St. Louis woman whom he met in Chicago in the spring of 1921 and whom he married that September. For their honeymoon he took her on a hunting trip to the wild northern Michigan lake region where he had spent his summer youth and where both of them promptly came down first with food poisoning and then with influenza.[5]

Met in the spring and married in the fall of 1921? A hunting trip? Food poisoning and influenza? Wet hair at the wedding? A late bride? A late bridegroom? Of all the people who attended the wedding, only one person now alive can answer the many questions and discrepancies which arise from the many versions of the same event. The groom is no longer alive, but the bride, who was eight years older than he, still is.

Hadley, now Mrs. Paul Scott Mowrer, lives in Chocorua, New Hampshire. Her hair is still brown and has a slight reddish cast to it in the sun. Hadley Mowrer's face is ruddy, unlined, and the small, pert nose of the photographs taken in the twenties remains unchanged. When she was interviewed in the spring of 1964, she wore a simple cotton dress. The sturdy, white shoes she was wearing were in direct contrast to her long, girlish legs. As she sat in an L. L. Bean chair with the full sunlight upon her, she seemed much younger than her then seventy-three years. In her own words, the former Mrs. Ernest Hemingway gave her account of the wedding, which dispels many of the conflicts in the previous eye witness accounts.

"Where did 'Tati,' which was your nickname for Ernest, and 'Hash,' which I believe he called you, come from?" I asked.

" 'Tati' was just one of my nicknames for him. 'Hash' came from 'Hash-a-Dad,' meaning the first three letters of Hadley, which was the name the girls at school gave me. Pig-Latin, I think it was called."

"Where did you go to school?"

"I went to Mary Institute in St. Louis and then to Bryn Mawr. I flunked out of Bryn Mawr though."

"It's funny that all of Ernest's wives, except Mary Welsh, were from St. Louis," I remarked.

"Yes, I knew Pauline in Paris, not in St. Louis at all. But then once when I was in upper school at Mary Institute, all of the little girls from the lower school came into the assembly hall and stood up against the wall. One pretty, little girl with long, blond hair stood out from the rest. That was Marty Gellhorn. Then, of course, Mary Welsh was working for the Chicago *Daily News* when Paul was editor. I think she was working on the women's section. Paul always said that she was a very good interviewer."

"You met Ernest in Chicago, didn't you?"

"Yes, I met him at Y. K. Smith's apartment at 100 East Chicago Avenue. My close friend, Kate Smith, who later married John Dos Passos, wanted me to come up to Chicago to the Three Arts Club. My mother had just died, and Kate asked me up out of sympathy and my need for distraction. I stayed with Y. K. and his wife, Doodles. Y. K. Smith was Kate's brother. A lot of young people hung out at his apartment, because Y. K. was such good company. The evening that we went over, a great train of young people appeared, and Ernest was one of them. I noticed Ernest right away, because he was so attractive. Ernest told someone years later that when I came into the room and was standing in the doorway, he knew that I was the girl he was going to marry. I don't know how true that story is, though; he never told it to me."

"I can remember reading it in Leicester Hemingway's book, *My Brother, Ernest Hemingway*," I added. "That was the springtime when you met him, and you were married in Horton Bay, Michigan, in September?"

"It was late August or early September that we met, and a year later we were married. My parents were not alive, and the Smiths and their aunt and uncle, Doctor and

'Auntie' Charles, were like second parents to me. Ernest loved the Charleses and that part of Michigan, so we decided to be married up there. Bill Smith, who was the Charleses' nephew and our best man, came over and lived in Paris when we were there. He was always a close friend of both of ours."

"What was the wedding like?"

"I had a beautiful wedding dress made. It was a small and very simple wedding. We had wonderful weather, a nice, clear day, as I remember. We were married in the little Methodist Church there, and then the whole wedding party and guests went across the road to the Dilworths', where we had a wedding breakfast. I just remembered a funny thing. When Ernest and I were coming out of the church, he stepped on my white, satin slippers. I thought at the time that it was a bad omen, and I guess it was."

"Did you stay at the Hemingway cottage or go camping on your honeymoon?"

"We stayed at the Hemingway cottage, because they had gone back to Oak Park. Ernest and I had a very poor honeymoon. We both had terrible colds. All that I can remember, when we first went to the cottage, was being sick. The Hemingways lent us a motorboat to use, but we didn't get to use it much, because we were both so miserable. The cottage seemed to have miles of rooms in it, but I'm sure that is just the way that I remember it. We had good weather the whole time and kept a nice open fire. We jugged wine over the fire by fermenting raisins, since it was still prohibition. When we got over our colds, we went into Petoskey. Ernest took me from house to house introducing me to all of his old girls, I especially remember one girl, a very pretty, dark-haired girl, [*this was probably Grace Quinlan*] who just stood by her kitchen table the whole time we visited her. She looked so embarrassed and ill at ease. I think that she really had a crush on Ernest."

"Did you fish in Michigan or meet any of Ernest's Indian friends?"

"I went fishing before our wedding with the George Breakers at Bent's Eagle River Camp in Wisconsin and from there we all went down to Horton Bay for the wedding. No, I never met any Indians while we were staying there. I have never been back to Horton Bay since then."

Hadley never went back to northern Michigan after her wedding and honeymoon. Neither did Ernest Hemingway, for any extended visit. He left his youthful haunts behind him, where they belonged: in his boyhood.

When Hemingway became famous, the people in "his part of Michigan" kept looking for him and hoping he would return. Some people had seen a "grizzled, old man with a white beard" who had asked for directions to the Hemingway cottage, "because everything had changed." The summer people, who buy their groceries in the general store in Horton Bay, are told about the times when Ernest Hemingway used to sit on the front porch "and listen to the cracker-barrel philosophers who gathered there."

Only one person, "Dutch" Pailthorp, actually talked with Hemingway when he drove through Petoskey sometime in the early 1950's. The two friends had dinner at the Pailthorps' modern house on the shore of Little Traverse Bay, which has a view of Petoskey, Harbor Springs, and Lake Michigan. "Dutch" Pailthorp asked Hemingway, who was on his way to Ketchum to finish a book, whether he would ever return to live in northern Michigan.

"No," Hemingway answered. "It's too civilized now."

Pailthorp was not satisfied with Hemingway's answer; he thought that the real reason was that there were too many bad memories connected with the region, beginning with Ernest's unhappy childhood and continuing through to his father's suicide. Hemingway, in his truthfulness, probably meant exactly what he said, for the region had changed from one of frontier conditions to a civilized resort area.

Ernest Hemingway always had the courage to leave behind him the places he loved and wrote about. He was always forced to leave the places which were the settings for his best writing. The Michigan of his early writings was abandoned. The Europe of *The Sun Also Rises* and *A Farewell to Arms* was renounced for Key West, Florida. The Spain of *For Whom the Bell Tolls* was lost. Even the Cuba of *The Old Man and the Sea* had to be relinquished.

Whenever the older writer returned to the settings of his earlier excellent fiction and tried to recapture the events again, something terrible happened: Hemingway seemed to be writing a cruel parody of himself. His novel *Across the River and Into the Trees*, which went back to the scene of *A Farewell to Arms* and "A Way You'll Never Be," was unsuccessful. In *The Dangerous Summer*, which destroyed even Hemingway aficionados' taste for bullfights and Spain, he had lost the key of *The Sun Also Rises* and *For Whom the Bell Tolls*. But the miracle occurred in Ketchum, Idaho (which he had never written about), where he wrote most of *A Moveable Feast*. Hemingway had gone back to the Paris of the twenties, via his own notes found in Paris, and captured it in his last book.

In *A Moveable Feast* Hemingway comments on his writing about Michigan and Paris:

> *Maybe away from Paris I could write about Paris as in Paris I could write about Michigan. I did not know it was too early for that because I did not know Paris well enough. But that was how it worked out eventually.*[6]

And Hemingway wrote well about Paris, as he had written earlier about his Michigan: northern Michigan.

Notes

Chapter I. "The Michigan Years"

1. Philip Young, *Ernest Hemingway* (New York: Rinehart and Company, Inc., 1952), p. 108.
2. Leicester Hemingway, *My Brother, Ernest Hemingway* (Cleveland and New York: The World Publishing Company, 1961), p. 23.
3. Charles A. Fenton, *The Apprenticeship of Ernest Hemingway: The Early Years* (New York: The Viking Press, 1958), p. 49.
4. Carlos Baker, *Hemingway: The Writer as Artist* (Princeton, New Jersey: Princeton University Press, 1956), p. 5.
5. William Forrest Dawson, "Ernest Hemingway: Petoskey Interview," *Michigan Alumnus Quarterly Review*, LXIV (March 1, 1958), p. 117.

Chapter II. History of Northern Michigan

1. *The Traverse Region* (Chicago: H. R. Page & Co., 1884), p. 16.
2. Catherine L. Stebbins, *Here I Shall Finish My Voyage! —Jacques Marquette* (Omena, Michigan: Solle's Press, 1960), p. 30.
3. *The Traverse Region*, p. 19.
4. *Ibid.*, p. 21.

Chapter III. Grandparents and Early Memories

1. Marcelline Hemingway Sanford, *At the Hemingways* (Boston and Toronto: Little, Brown and Company, 1961), p. 3.
2. Leicester Hemingway, *My Brother, Ernest Hemingway* (Cleveland and New York: The World Publishing Company, 1961), p. 26.

3. Marcelline Hemingway Sanford, *op. cit.*, p. 21.
4. *Ibid.*, p. 4.

Chapter IV. Three High School Stories

1. Charles A. Fenton, *The Apprenticeship of Ernest Hemingway: The Early Years* (New York: The Viking Press, 1958), p. 18.
2. *Ibid.*

Chapter V. The Indian Camp

1. Carlos Baker, *Hemingway: The Writer as Artist* (Princeton, New Jersey: Princeton University Press, 1956), p. 23.
2. William Forrest Dawson, "Ernest Hemingway: Petoskey Interview," *Michigan Alumnus Quarterly Review*, LXIV (March 1, 1958), p. 21.
3. Leicester Hemingway, *My Brother, Ernest Hemingway* (Cleveland and New York: The World Publishing Company, 1961), pp. 42–43.
4. Ernest Hemingway, *The Short Stories of Ernest Hemingway* (New York: Charles Scribner's Sons, 1938), p. 92.
5. *Ibid.*

Chapter VI. Doctor and Mrs. Hemingway

1. Charles Fenton, *The Apprenticeship of Ernest Hemingway: The Early Years* (New York: The Viking Press, 1958), p. 13.
2. George Plimpton, "Interview—The Art of Fiction XXI," *Paris Review*, XVIII (October, 1958), p. 82.
3. Carlos Baker, "A Search for the Man As He Really Was," *The New York Times Book Review* (July 26, 1964), p. 14.
4. Leicester Hemingway, *My Brother, Ernest Hemingway* (Cleveland and New York: The World Publishing Company, 1961), p. 92.
5. Ernest Hemingway, *The Short Stories of Ernest Hemingway* (New York: Charles Scribner's Sons, 1938), p. 101.
6. William F. Dawson, "Ernest Hemingway: Petoskey Interview," *Michigan Alumnus Quarterly Review* LXIV (March 1, 1958), p. 118.
7. Marcelline Hemingway Sanford, *At the Hemingways* (Boston and Toronto: Little, Brown and Company, 1961), p. 54.
8. William F. Dawson, *op. cit.*, p. 120.
9. Marcelline Hemingway Sanford, *op. cit.*, p. 58.
10. Ernest Hemingway, *op. cit.*, p. 490.
11. *Ibid.*, p. 491.

12. Malcolm Cowley, "A Portrait of Mister Papa," *Ernest Hemingway: The Man and His Work*, ed., John K. M. McCaffery (Cleveland and New York: The World Publishing Company, 1950), p. 43. Originally published in *Life*, January 10, 1949.

Chapter VII. Riding the Rails

1. Malcolm Cowley, "A Portrait of Mister Papa," *Ernest Hemingway: The Man and His Work*, ed., John K. M. McCaffery (Cleveland and New York: The World Publishing Company, 1950), p. 46.
2. Marcelline Hemingway Sanford, *At the Hemingways* (Boston and Toronto: Little, Brown and Company, 1961), p. 150.
3. Ernest Hemingway, *The Short Stories of Ernest Hemingway* (New York: Charles Scribner's Sons, 1938), p. 131.
4. *Ibid.*, p. 386.
5. Marcelline Hemingway Sanford, *op. cit.*, p. 73.
6. Carlos Baker, *Hemingway, the Writer as Artist* (Princeton, New Jersey: Princeton University Press, 1956), p. 140.
7. Ernest Hemingway, "Remembering Shooting Flying," *Esquire*, Vol. 3 (February, 1935), p. 21.

Chapter VIII. The Bacons and Prudence

1. George Plimpton, "Interview—The Art of Fiction XXI," *Paris Review*, XVIII (October, 1958), p. 79.
2. Theodore Bardacke, "Hemingway's Women," *Ernest Hemingway: The Man and His Work*, ed., John K. M. McCaffery (Cleveland and New York: The World Publishing Company, 1950), p. 348.
3. Ernest Hemingway, *The Short Stories of Ernest Hemingway* (New York: Charles Scribner's Sons, 1938), p. 498.

Chapter IX. War Wounds

1. Malcolm Cowley, "A Portrait of Mister Papa," *Ernest Hemingway: The Man and His Work*, ed., John K. M. McCaffery (Cleveland and New York: The World Publishing Company, 1950), p. 47.
2. George Plimpton, "Interview—Ernest Hemingway," *Writers at Work: Second Series*, ed. George Plimpton (New York: The Viking Press, 1963), p. 230.
3. William Forrest Dawson, "Ernest Hemingway: Petoskey Interview," *Michigan Alumnus Quarterly Review*, LXIV (March 1, 1958), p. 117.

Chapter X. Horton Bay

1. Carlos Baker, *Hemingway: The Writer as Artist* (Princeton, New Jersey: Princeton University Press, 1956), p. 7.
2. Charles Fenton, *The Apprenticeship of Ernest Hemingway: The Early Years* (New York: The Viking Press, 1954), p. 109.
3. Charlevoix County Historical Program (1935), p. 40.
4. Marcelline Hemingway Sanford, *At the Hemingways* (Boston and Toronto: Little, Brown and Company, 1961), p. 216.
5. Ernest Hemingway, *The Short Stories of Ernest Hemingway* (New York: Charles Scribner's Sons, 1938), p. 82.
6. *Ibid.*
7. *Ibid.*
8. *Ibid.*
9. *Ibid.*
10. Ernest Hemingway, "An Old Newsman Writes," *Esquire*, Vol. II (December, 1934), p. 25.

Chapter XI. Marjorie and Bill

1. George Hemphill, "Hemingway and James," *Kenyon Review*, Vol. XI (Winter, 1949), p. 333.
2. *Ibid.*
3. *Ibid.*
4. Ernest Hemingway, *The Short Stories of Ernest Hemingway* (New York: Charles Scribner's Sons, 1938), p. 107.
5. *Ibid.*
6. Charlevoix County Historical Society Program (1935), p. 46.
7. Ernest Hemingway, *op. cit.*, p. 110.
8. *Ibid.*
9. William F. Dawson, "Ernest Hemingway: Petoskey Interview," *Michigan Alumnus Quarterly Review*, LXIV (March 1, 1958), p. 122.
10. Howard Loeb, *the way it was* (New York: Criterion Books, 1959), p. 247.
11. *Ibid.*, p. 121.
12. *Ibid.*, p. 122.
13. *Ibid.*
14. *Ibid.*, p. 123.
15. *Ibid.*
16. *Ibid.*, p. 122.
17. *Ibid.*
18. *Ibid.*

19. *Ibid.*
20. *Ibid.*, p. 124.
21. *Ibid.*, p. 125.
22. *Ibid.*
23. *Ibid.*, p. 125.
24. *Ibid.*
25. Leicester Hemingway, *My Brother, Ernest Hemingway* (Cleveland and New York: The World Publishing Company, 1961), p. 67.

Chapter XII. Two-Hearted Rivers

1. Leicester Hemingway, *My Brother, Ernest Hemingway* (Cleveland and New York: The World Publishing Company, 1961), pp. 92–93.
2. Allen Tate, "Review of Big Two-Hearted River," *Nation*, Vol. CXXII (February 10, 1926), pp. 160–162.
3. F. S. Fitzgerald, "How to Waste Material: A Note on My Generation," *Bookman*, LXIII (May, 1926), pp. 262–265.
4. Malcolm Cowley, introd., *The Portable Hemingway* (New York: The Viking Press, 1944), p. XIX.
5. Sheridan Baker, "Hemingway's Two-Hearted River," *Michigan Alumnus Quarterly Review*, LXV (February 28, 1959), p. 148.
6. Charles Fenton, *The Apprenticeship of Ernest Hemingway: The Early Years* (New York: The Viking Press, 1954), p. 158.
7. Ernest Hemingway to Gertrude Stein, August 15, 1924, *The Flowers of Friendship: Letters Written to Gertrude Stein*, ed., Donald Gallup (New York: Alfred A. Knopf, 1953), p. 164.
8. Ernest Hemingway, *The Short Stories of Ernest Hemingway* (New York: Charles Scribner's Sons, 1938), p. 210.
9. *Ibid.*, p. 213.
10. *Ibid.*
11. *Ibid.*, p. 215.
12. *Ibid.*, p. 217.
13. *Ibid.*, p. 218.
14. *Ibid.*, p. 221.
15. *Ibid.*, p. 222.
16. *Ibid.*, p. 224.
17. *Ibid.*, p. 227.
18. Ernest Hemingway to Gertrude Stein, *op. cit.*, p. 165.

Chapter XIII. Petoskey

1. Carlos Baker, *Hemingway: The Writer as Artist* (Princeton, New Jersey: Princeton University Press, 1956), p. 43.
2. *Ibid.*, p. 420.
3. Ernest Hemingway, *The Torrents of Spring, The Hemingway Reader*, ed. Charles Poore (New York: Charles Scribner's Sons, 1953), p. 42.
4. *Ibid.*
5. *Ibid.*, p. 59.
6. *Ibid.*, p. 65.
7. *Ibid.*, p. 84.
8. *Ibid.*, p. 72.

Chapter XIV. Twenty-first Birthday

1. Leicester Hemingway, *My Brother, Ernest Hemingway* (Cleveland and New York: The World Publishing Company, 1961), p. 23.
2. *Ibid.*, p. 64.
3. *Ibid.*, p. 65.
4. *Ibid.*
5. *Ibid.*
6. *Ibid.*, p. 66.
7. *Ibid.*, p. 67.
8. *Ibid.*
9. *Ibid.*
10. *Ibid.*, p. 68.
11. *Ibid.*, p. 69.

Chapter XV. Michigan Wedding

1. Associated Press, "Hemingway Rites Await Son," *New York Journal-American* (July 3, 1961).
2. Marcelline Sanford Hemingway, *At the Hemingways* (Boston and Toronto: Little, Brown and Company, 1961), p. 209.
3. Leicester Hemingway, *My Brother, Ernest Hemingway* (Cleveland and New York: The World Publishing Company, 1961), p. 72.
4. *Ibid.*, p. 74.
5. Alfred G. Aronowitz and Pete Hamill, "The Hemingway Story," Article X, *The New York Post* (July 14, 1961).
6. Ernest Hemingway, *A Moveable Feast* (New York: Charles Scribner's Sons, 1964), p. 7.

Bibliography

Books by Hemingway

Three Stories and Ten Poems, Paris and Dijon: Contact Publishing Co., 1923.

in our time, Paris: Three Mountains Press, 1924.

In Our Time, New York: Boni and Liveright, 1925.

The Torrents of Spring, New York: Charles Scribner's Sons, 1926.

Today Is Friday, Englewood, N.J.: As Stauble Publishing Co., 1926.

The Sun Also Rises, New York: Charles Scribner's Sons, 1926.

Men without Women, New York: Charles Scribner's Sons, 1952.

A Farewell to Arms, New York: Charles Scribner's Sons, 1929.

The Collected Poems of Ernest Hemingway, Paris: The Library of Living Poetry, 1929.

Death in the Afternoon, New York: Charles Scribner's Sons, 1932.

Winner Take Nothing, New York: Charles Scribner's Sons, 1933.

Green Hills of Africa, New York: Charles Scribner's Sons, 1935.

To Have and Have Not, New York: Charles Scribner's Sons, 1935.

The Spanish Earth, Cleveland: The J. B. Savage Co., 1938.

The Spanish War, London: Fact, 1938.

The Short Stories of Ernest Hemingway, "Scribner's Text Edition," New York: Charles Scribner's Sons, 1938.

The Fifth Column and the First Forty-Nine Stories, New York: Charles Scribner's Sons, 1938.

For Whom the Bell Tolls, New York: Charles Scribner's Sons, 1940.

Across the River and into the Trees, New York: Charles Scribner's Sons, 1950.

The Old Man and the Sea, New York: Charles Scribner's Sons, 1952.
The Hemingway Reader, ed., CHARLES POORE, New York: Charles Scribner's Sons, 1953.
A Moveable Feast, New York: Charles Scribner's Sons, 1964.

Articles by Hemingway

"Fishing for Trout in a Sporting Way," *Toronto Star Weekly*, April 24, 1920, p. 13.
"When You Camp Out Do It Right," *Toronto Star Weekly*, June 26, 1920, p. 17.
"When You Go Camping Take Lots of Skeeter Dope and Don't Ever Lose It," *Toronto Star Weekly*, August 5, 1920, p. 11.
"The Best Rainbow Trout Fishing in the World is at the Canadian Soo," *Toronto Star Weekly*, August 28, 1920, p. 21.
"A Fight with a 20-Pound Trout," *Toronto Star Weekly*, November 20, 1920.
"An Old Newsman Writes," *Esquire*, II (December, 1934), 25–26.
"Remembering Shooting Flying," *Esquire*, III (February, 1935), 21.
"A.D. Southern Style," *Esquire*, III (May, 1935), 25.
"Monologue to the Maestro," *Esquire*, IV (October, 1935), 21 ff.
"The Malady of Power," *Esquire*, IV (November, 1935), 31.

Books about and Pertaining to Hemingway

ANDERSON, SHERWOOD. *Letters of Sherwood Anderson*. Boston: Little, Brown and Company, 1953.
————. *Sherwood Anderson's Memoirs*. New York: Harcourt, Brace and Co., 1942.
ATKINS, J. A. *The Art of Ernest Hemingway: His Work and Personality*. London: P. Nevill, 1952.
BAKER, CARLOS HEARD. *Hemingway, the Writer as Artist*. Princeton, N.J.: Princeton University Press, 1956.
———— (ed.). *Hemingway and His Critics: An International Anthology*. ("American Century Series"), New York: Hill and Wang, 1961.
BRINNIN, JOHN MALCOLM. *The Third Rose: Gertrude Stein and Her World*. Boston and Toronto: Little, Brown and Co., 1959.
CALLAGHAN, MORLEY. *That Summer in Paris*. New York: Dell Publishing Co., June, 1964.
CAPA, ROBERT. *Slightly Out of Focus*. New York: Henry Holt and Company, 1947.
CHASE, RICHARD. *The American Novel and Its Tradition*. Garden City, N.Y.: Doubleday and Co., Inc., 1957.

Cody, Morrill. *Hemingway's Paris.* (As told to Morrill Cody by James Charter's "The Barman.") "A Tower Book." New York: Macaulay Co., 1965.

Cowden, Roy W. (ed.). *The Writer and His Craft* ("Ann Arbor Books"), Ann Arbor, Mich.: University of Michigan Press, 1959.

Cowley, Malcolm. *Exile's Return.* New York: The Viking Press, 1956.

Fenton, Charles A. *The Apprenticeship of Ernest Hemingway: The Early Years.* New York: Farrar, Straus, and Young, 1954.

Gallup, Donald (ed.). *The Flowers of Friendship: Letters Written to Gertrude Stein.* New York: Alfred A. Knopf, 1953.

Gregory, Horace (ed.). *The Portable Sherwood Anderson.* With an introduction by Horace Gregory. New York: The Viking Press, 1949.

Hanrahan, Gene Z. (ed.). *The Wild Years: Ernest Hemingway.* With an introduction by Gene Z. Hanrahan. New York: Dell Publishing Co., Inc., 1962.

Hemingway, Leicester. *My Brother, Ernest Hemingway.* Cleveland and New York: The World Publishing Company, 1961, 1962.

Hicks, Granville (ed.). *The Living Novel: A Symposium.* New York: The Macmillan Company, 1957.

Knoll, Robert E. (ed.). *McAlmon and the Lost Generation: A Self-Portrait.* With a commentary by Robert E. Knoll. Lincoln, Nebraska: University of Nebraska Press, 1962.

Kiley, Jed. *Hemingway: An Old Friend Remembers.* New York: Hawthorn Books, Inc., 1965.

Lania, Leo. *Hemingway: A Pictorial Biography.* ("A Studio Book"), New York: The Viking Press, 1961.

Loeb, Harold. *the way it was.* New York: Criterion Books, 1959.

Machlin, Milt. *The Private Hell of Hemingway.* New York: Paperback Library, Inc., 1962.

McCaffery, John K. M. (ed.). *Ernest Hemingway, the Man and His Work.* Cleveland: World Publishing Co., 1956.

Sanderson, S. F. *Ernest Hemingway.* New York: Grove Press, Inc., 1961.

Sanford, Marcelline Hemingway. *At the Hemingways: A Family Portrait.* Boston: Little, Brown and Co., 1961, 1962.

Scherman, David E. and Redlich, Rosemarie. *Literary America.* New York: Dodd, Mead & Co., 1952.

SCRIGGE, ELIZABETH. *Gertrude Stein, Her Life and Work.* New York: Harper and Brothers, 1957.

STEIN, GERTRUDE. *The Autobiography of Alice B. Toklas.* New York: Harcourt, Brace and Co., 1933.

———. *Selected Writings of Gertrude Stein,* ed., CARL VAN VECHTEN. New York: Random House, 1946.

WEEKS, ROBERT P. (ed.). *Hemingway: A Collection of Critical Essays.* Englewood Cliffs, N.J.: Prentice-Hall, Inc., 1962.

WILSON, COLIN. *The Outsider.* London: Victor Gollancz, Ltd., 1956, pp. 31–39.

YOUNG, PHILIP. *Ernest Hemingway.* New York: Rinehart, 1952.

———. Ernest Hemingway. ("Pamphlets on American Writers" [No. 17].) Minneapolis, Minn.: University of Minnesota Press, 1959.

Articles about Hemingway

ALKINS, JOHN. "Hemingway and the American Novel," *Wisdom Magazine,* twenty-sixth issue, June, 1958.

BAKER, CARLOS. "A Search for the Man as He Really Was," *The New York Times Book Review,* July 26, 1964, p. 14.

———. "Hemingway," *Saturday Review,* July 29, 1961, p. 10.

BAKER, SHERIDAN. "Hemingway's Two-Hearted River," *Michigan Alumnus Quarterly Review,* LXV (February 28, 1959), pp. 142–144.

BETSKY, SEYMOUR. "The World Weighs a Writer's Influence: A Last Visit," *Saturday Review,* July 29, 1961, p. 22.

BISHOP, JOHN PEALE. "The Missing All," *Virginia Quarterly Review,* XIII (Winter, 1937), pp. 107–121.

BOYD, ERNEST. Review of *Torrents of Spring, Independent,* CXVI (June 12, 1926), 694.

BURGUM, E. B. "Hemingway's Development," *New Masses,* XXIX (November 22, 1938), 21–23.

CIARDI, JOHN. "Manner of Speaking: Language of an Age," *Saturday Review,* July 29, 1961, p. 32.

COWLEY, MALCOLM. "Hemingway and the Hero," *New Republic,* CI (December 4, 1944), 754–758.

———. "Hemingway at Midnight," *New Republic,* CXI (August 14, 1944), 190.

———. Introduction to *The Portable Hemingway.* New York: The Viking Press, 1944.

———. "A Portrait of Mister Papa," *Life,* XXVI (January 10, 1949), 86–101.

DAWSON, WILLIAM FORREST. "Ernest Hemingway: Petoskey Interview," *Michigan Alumnus Quarterly Review*, LXIV (Winter, 1958), 114–123.

DE MADARIAGA, SALVADOR. "The World Weigh's a Writer's Influence: Spain," *Saturday Review*, July 29, 1961, p. 18.

DOLBIER, MAURICE. " 'Ernest Hemingway,' " review of *My Brother, Ernest Hemingway*, New York *Herald Tribune*, February 27, 1962.

EHRENBURG, ILYA. "The World Weighs a Writer's Influence: USSR," *Saturday Review*, July 29, 1961, p. 20.

FITZGERALD, F. S. "How To Waste Material: A Note on My Generation," *Bookman*, LXIII (May, 1926), 262–265.

FROHOCK, W. M. "Ernest Hemingway: Violence and Discipline," *Southwest Review*. XXXII (Winter and Spring, 1947), 89–97, 184–193.

GALANTIERE, L. "The Brushwood Boy at the Front," *Hound and Horn*, III (January–March, 1930), 259–262.

HALLIDAY, E. M. "Hemingway's In Our Time," *Explicator*, VII (March, 1949), 35.

HEMPHILL, GEORGE. "Hemingway and James," *Kenyon Review*, XI (Winter, 1949), 50–60.

KASHKEEN, J. "A Tragedy of Craftsmanship," *International Literature* (U.S.S.R.), 1935, No. 5.

LEVI, CARLO. "The World Weighs a Writer's Influence: Italy," *Saturday Review*, July 29, 1961, p. 19.

LOEB, HAROLD. "The Young Writer in Paris and Pamplona," *Saturday Review*, July 29, 1961, p. 25.

LYONS, LEONARD. "Trade Winds," *Saturday Review*, July 29, 1961, p. 6.

MORAES, FRANK. "The World Weighs a Writer's Influence: India," *Saturday Review*, July 29, 1961, p. 18.

PLIMPTON, GEORGE. "The Art of Fiction XXI, Ernest Hemingway," *Paris Review*, XVIII (Spring, 1958), 61–82.

———. "Interview—Ernest Hemingway," *Writers at Work: Second Series*. Ed., GEORGE PLIMPTON. New York: The Viking Press, 1963, p. 230.

PRYCE-JONES, ALAN. "The World Weighs a Writer's Influence: England," *Saturday Review*, July 29, 1961, p. 21.

R., M. "Review," *transatlantic review*, April, 1924, pp. 247–248.

ROSS, LILLIAN, "How Do You Like It Now, Gentlemen?" *New Yorker*, XXVI (May 13, 1950), 36–62.

———. "Portrait of Hemingway," Preface to *Reporting*. New York: Simon and Schuster, 1964, p. 187.

SCHWARTZ, DELMORE. "Ernest Hemingway's Literary Situation," *Southern Review*, III (April, 1938), 769–782.

STEIN, GERTRUDE. "Ernest Hemingway and the Post-War Decade," *Atlantic* CLII (August, 1933), 197–208.

TATE, ALLEN. "Review of Big Two-Hearted River," *Nation*, CXXII (February 10, 1926) 160–162.

———. "The Spirituality of Roughnecks," review of *Torrents of Spring*, *Nation* CXXIII (July 28, 1926), 89.

UREST, ORTON. "Some Notes Bibliographical and Otherwise on the Books of Ernest Hemingway," *Publisher's Weekly*, CXVII (February 15, 1930), 884–886.

WILSON, EDMUND. "Ernest Hemingway, Bourbon Gauge of Morale," *Atlantic Monthly*, CLXIII (July, 1939), 36–46.

Newspaper Articles
at the Time of Hemingway's Death

ALTSCHULER, HARRY. "Papa Oft Looked Death in the Face," *New York Mirror*, July 4, 1961.

ANDERSON, JAMES C. (United Press International). "Hemingway Inquest Hinges on Questioning of His Wife," *New York World-Telegram and Sun*, July 3, 1961, 1.

ARONOWITZ, ALFRED G. and HAMILL, PETE. "Hemingway's Legacy · Words," *New York Post*, July 13, 1961.

ARONOWITZ, ALFRED G. and HAMILL, PETE. "The Hemingway Story," *New York Post* (eleven articles), July 3, 1961–July 16, 1961.

ASSOCIATED PRESS. "Hemingway Rites Await Son," *New York Journal-American*, July 5, 1961.

ASSOCIATED PRESS. "Hemingway's Funeral Waits Arrival of Son from Africa," *New York Post*, July 5, 1961.

ASSOCIATED PRESS. "Services for 'Papa': No Eulogy," *New York Post*, July 6, 1961, 3.

ASSOCIATED PRESS. "Wife in Cuba for Talk on Hemingway Shrine," *New York Post*, July 24, 1961.

BROMBERG, LESTER. "Mr. Hemingway, the Fighter," *New York World-Telegram and Sun*," July 3, 1961.

COWLEY, MALCOLM. "One Man's Hemingway," *New York Herald Tribune*, July 9, 1961, 3.

FEINGOLD, SIDNEY. "The Writer: Blood, Guts and Genius," *New York Daily News*, July 3, 1961, 3.

KOBER, BARBARA. "JFK Leads World Tribute," *New York Journal-American*, July 3, 1961, 4.

LERNER, MAX. "Papa," *New York Post*, July 3, 1961, 19.

LYONS, LEONARD. "I Remember Papa," "The Lyons Den," *New York Post*, July 3, 1961, 3.

LYONS, LEONARD. "The Lyons Den," *New York Post*, July 22, 1961.

MARTIN, RON. "Author's Boyhood in State Recalled," *The Detroit Free Press*, July 3, 1961, 1.

POORE, CHARLES. "Books: Hemingway," *The New York Times*, July 3, 1961, 6.

ROBBINS, ALFRED. "A Final Farewell to Arms for Ernest Hemingway," *New York Journal-American*, July 3, 1961, 4.

RUARK, ROBERT C. "Papa's Death Reaches Africa," *New York World-Telegram and Sun*, July 6, 1961.

RUARK, ROBERT C. "This Safari Is for Ernest," *New York World-Telegram and Sun*, July 7, 1961.

SOBEL, LOUIS. " 'Papa' Was Newsmen's Pet," *New York Journal-American*, July 6, 1961.

UNITED PRESS INTERNATIONAL. "Ordonez Kills Two Bulls in Honor of Hemingway," *The New York Times*, July 4, 1961.

UNITED PRESS INTERNATIONAL. "Was Papa Suicide? We May Never Learn," *New York Daily News*, July 4, 1961.

UNITED PRESS INTERNATIONAL. "Hemingway Buried with Catholic Rites," *New York Journal-American*, July 6, 1961.

UNITED PRESS INTERNATIONAL. "Ernest Hemingway Buried Near His Home in Idaho," *New York Herald Tribune*, July 7, 1961.

WHITE, WILLIAM S. " 'Papa's' Death a Sad Blow," *New York Journal-American*, July 5, 1961.

WILSON, EARL. " 'Papa' Couldn't Spell . . . ," "It Happened Last Night," *New York Post*, July 5, 1961.

WINCHELL, WALTER, "A Farewell to Hemingway," *New York Mirror*, July 6 1961.

"The Bell Tolls for Hemingway," *New York Daily News*, July 3, 1961, 18–19.

"The Bell Tolls for Ernest Hemingway," *New York Post*, July 3, 1961, 3.

"Death in the Morning Ends Hemingway Story," *New York Journal-American*, July 3, 1961, 13.

"Hemingway Killed By Shot: 'Accident,' " *New York Herald Tribune*, July 3, 1961.

"Hemingway, Master Stylist, Wrote 'As Truly as I Could,' " *New York World-Telegram and Sun*, July 3, 1961, 3.

"Hemingway's Prize-Winning Works Reflected Preoccupation with Life and Death," *The New York Times*, July 3, 1961, 6.

"Life of Hemingway: Works Controversial," *New York Herald Tribune*, July 3, 1961.

"The President's Eulogy," *New York Post*, July 3, 1961, 3.

"France Shocked Over Hemingway," *The New York Times*, July 4, 1961.

"Hemingway Inquest Is Ruled Out after Authorities Talk to Family," *The New York Times*, July 4, 1961.

"Coast Paper Claims Hemingway a Suicide," *New York Journal-American*, July 7, 1961.

"Authors: 'The Bell Tolls,' " *Newsweek*, July 10, 1961, 32.

"A Hemingway Treasure Chest," *The New York Times Book Review*, July 16, 1961, 2.

Books of General Interest

ALLEN, FREDERICK LEWIS. *Only Yesterday*, New York: Bantam Books, 1950.

BLACKBIRD, ANDREW J. *History of the Ottawa and Chippewa Indians of Michigan*, 1887.

Charlevoix County Historical Program, 1935.

CRANE, STEPHEN. *The Red Badge of Courage* ("The Pocket Library"), New York: Pocket Books, Inc., 1954.

DUNBAR, WILLIS FREDERICK. *Michigan: A History of the Wolverine State*, Grand Rapids, Michigan: William B. Eerdman Publishing Co., 1965.

FIELDING, HENRY. *The History of the Adventures of Joseph Andrews (and of his friend Mr. Abraham Adams)*, New York: The Modern Library, 1930.

HEDRICK, U. P. *The Land of the Crooked Tree*, New York: Oxford University Press, 1948.

HENRY, ALEXANDER. *Travels and Adventures in Canada and the Indian Territories between 1760 and 1776*, 1809.

PARKMAN, FRANCIS. *The Jesuits in North America*, Boston: Little, Brown and Co., 1867 and 1963.

POWERS, PERRY F. *A History of Northern Michigan and Its People*, Volume I, Chicago: The Lewis Publishing Company, 1912.

SHURTLEFF, MARY BELLE. *Old Arbe Croche*, A Factual and Comprehensive History of Cross Village, Michigan, 1963.

STEBBINS, CATHERINE L. *Here I Shall Finish My Voyage!—Jacques Marquette*, Omena, Mich.: Sollés Press, 1960.

The Traverse Region, Chicago: H. R. Page & Co., 1884.

TWAIN, MARK. *The Adventures of Huckleberry Finn*, New York: Harper and Brothers, 1959.

Acknowledgments

In the summer of 1960, I spent three months in northern Michigan comparing Ernest Hemingway's fictional descriptions of the countryside to the actual places. After interviewing people who had known Hemingway and his family in Michigan, I discovered that many of the fictional characters were drawn from life. Some even had the same or similar names in both fact and fiction.

The two people from Petoskey, Michigan, who helped me the most, were Edwin "Dutch" Pailthorp and the late Mrs. Joseph E. Otis, junior. My family had known "Dutch" Pailthorp for years, and he told me about the days when he was a close friend of Hemingway in Petoskey. Mrs. Otis, who died in 1964, had also known Hemingway when she was a teenager growing up in Petoskey. Mrs. Otis, the former Miss Grace Quinlan, kept many letters from Hemingway which she received in the early twenties. After her death, her son, Webster Otis, sent to me a copy of another Hemingway letter. The contents of the important letters gave Ernest Hemingway's point of view about Petoskey, his parents, girls, his attitude toward writing, sports, and his own independence, his first wife and Michigan wedding, plus clarifying several incidents which have been distorted through the memories of others.

Several other Petoskey residents gave lengthy inter-

views in 1960. Joseph Bacon, who is now ninety-five and still lives in Petoskey, was invaluable as a raconteur of tales about the Hemingway family and their neighbors. He was probably the inspiration for "Joe Garner" in "Ten Indians." Mr. Bacon had saved several photographs and the funeral pamphlet of Ernest Hemingway's grandfather which is included in this book. Owen White of Petoskey contributed information, even though he had pledged his photographs to the late Marcelline Hemingway Sanford. His brother, the late Kenneth White of Westport, Connecticut, was interviewed in 1963 in New York.

Mrs. Wesley Dilworth of Boyne City, Michigan, knew the whole Hemingway family and was able to give many insights into their family life. She knew about the early days of Horton Bay and added information and photographs which only a lifetime resident could have collected. Mrs. George Depew, Mrs. James Keltz, Mrs. Bauer, John McConnell, and Stanley Van Hoesen added background and information about the Hemingways at Walloon Lake and Horton Bay.

In 1963 I met Mrs. Ernest Hemingway in New York and showed her my material, photographs, and told her about further information gathered in other summers in Michigan and through research in the New York Public Library. She was both interested and helpful.

Mary Hemingway wrote a letter of introduction to Mrs. Paul Scott Mowrer, who had been the first Mrs. Ernest Hemingway. Hadley Mowrer answered many questions in a long interview in the spring of 1964 and later contributed other information, clippings, and photographs.

Mrs. Jasper J. Jepson, the former Ursula Hemingway, was kind enough to read my completed manuscript for inaccuracies. Her corrections, which she wrote in several letters, have been added to the text. Her sister, "Sunny" Hemingway Miller, gave a brief interview in 1960.

Beginning in 1960 I began my search for the original or copies of the three Hemingway high school stories included in this book. Since the original Tabulas had disappeared, my quest seemed hopeless. Finally in 1965 after many letters and telephone calls, Miss Lena E. Crawford, Librarian of the Oak Park and River Forest High School Library, sent the copies made from the original yearbooks kept in a vault. Mary Hemingway gave permission to include them in my book.

Laurie M. Brown, Librarian of the Harbor Springs Christian Association Library, provided information and books especially for the "History of Northern Michigan" chapter. Mr. and Mrs. David Irish of Harbor Springs have also helped by doing last-minute, on-the-spot research.

My stepfather, James McConnaughey, who is an author, editor, and newspaper publisher, helped me by doing some major editing on the second rough draft. My mother, Louise H. McConnaughey, lived through the initial, heavy research in the summer of 1960. She has visited all of the locations investigated for the book. My father-in-law, Raymond Montgomery, senior, drew the two regional maps identifying places mentioned in the text.

Nora Wainer has done the difficult job of copy editing and checking facts, plus adding valuable editorial knowledge and comment. Judith Gustafson and Patricia McVay did an excellent job of typing different versions of the manuscript.

My husband, Raymond A. Montgomery, junior, has probably had the most difficult task. Although his favorite author was, and is, Hemingway, it has been trying for him to come into a half-completed project when most of the fun of the original research is over and the work of rechecking, writing, and rewriting continued for years.

Waitsfield, Vermont
March, 1966

Index